Historical Archaeology

Volume 16, Numbers 1–2   1982

Journal of the
Society for Historical Archaeology

RONALD L. MICHAEL, Editor

Anthropology Section
California State College
California, Pennsylvania 15419

Published by
THE SOCIETY FOR HISTORICAL ARCHAEOLOGY

Identification of Manufacturers and Marks

William C. Gates, Jr.
Dana E. Ormerod

Historical Archaeology: Journal of the Society for Historical Archaeology
Volume 16, Nos. 1–2, 1982

The Society for Historical Archaeology

Historical Archaeology is published annually by the Society for Historical Archaeology. Subscription is by membership in the Society. Four times yearly members also receive the Society for Historical Archaeology *Newsletter*.

Membership in the Society is open to all, and dues are $20.00 (U.S.) annually for individuals and $40.00 (U.S.) for institutional membership.

Address all communications regarding membership and back issues to American Anthropological Association, 1703 New Hampshire Avenue, N.W., Washington, DC 20009. Make checks payable to the Society for Historical Archaeology.

Manuscripts submitted for publication should be sent to the *Editor*, Ronald Michael. Citation and reference style should follow that specified in *American Antiquity* 44(1): 199–204. Other author information can be found in this issue of *Historical Archaeology*. Books, lengthy articles, or films for review should be sent to the *Book Review Editor*, Roderick Sprague.

News items, notices of meetings, and other information for the *Newsletter* should be sent to the *Newsletter Editor*, Norman Barka.

Notification of new articles, books, or manuscripts dealing with historical archaeology should also be sent to the *Newsletter Editor*.

Contents

WILLIAM C. GATES, JR.
DANA E. ORMEROD

THE EAST LIVERPOOL POTTERY DISTRICT: IDENTIFICATION OF MANUFACTURERS AND MARKS

ABSTRACT

The potteries of the East Liverpool district were the largest domestic producers of ceramic toilet and table wares between 1890 and 1940. This volume is a study of the manufacturers and marks of that district. It includes a brief history of the local pottery industry from its inception in 1840 to the present, skeletal histories of 85 individual firms, and photographs of 993 known marks utilized by these companies. This treatise is designed to provide a reference for the identification and interpretation of archaeological data. It also contains peripheral appendices to facilitate effective use of the publication.

Introduction

The manufacturers of the East Liverpool, Ohio, pottery district have been the largest domestic producers of whiteware since 1895. Available publications do not provide adequate information on these manufacturers or their pottery marks. John Ramsay, in his *American Potters and Pottery*, said of the East Liverpool district ". . . in all, nearly a hundred individuals, partnerships, and corporations succeeded each other in various combinations. An attempt to chronicle them would be entirely too confusing. . ." (1939: 76). With the exception of Duke's edition (1977) on the Hall China Company, few publications since Barber's *Pottery and Porcelain of the United States* (1893) and *Marks of American Potters* (1904) have made a serious attempt to unravel the complexities of the region's pottery industry. In general, post-Barber publications have been repetitive paraphrasing which have perpetuated or generated, erroneous information resulting in further confusion about the East Liverpool pottery industry. These publications have attempted to chronicle ceramic producers on either a national or world-wide basis. This broad perspective has resulted in an incomplete and oversimplified treatment. When manufacturers' marks are included, they are usually artistically corrupted.

In recent years, archaeology has experienced increased activity related to 19th and 20th century research. This interest, to a large extent, is the result of federal guidelines as they relate to cultural resource management. Since ceramics are one of the largest classes of artifacts recovered from a historic archaeological site, a reliable data base is required in order to make effective interpretive judgements. A reliable body of reference material is necessary in order to identify the source of manufacture and the date of production of ceramics recovered from an excavation.

The dearth of accurate historical information concerning producers of late 19th and 20th century ceramics has caused archaeologists to refer to the data gap as the "whiteware problem." In order to alleviate some of the deficiencies in the data base of American pottery and porcelain during this period, this volume is a regional study of a major ceramic center. Although useful to collectors, curators, and other interested individuals, the major purpose of the treatise is to provide a reference for the identification and interpretation of archaeological data. It is not claimed to be definitive in terms of text or the pottery marks. However, the information contained in this publication is the result of the intensive research of available resources. It is the most thorough treatment of the East Liverpool pottery district to date.

The East Liverpool district encompasses the geographic area immediately surrounding East Liverpool and includes the towns of Wellsville, Ohio, and Chester and Newell, West Virginia, directly across the Ohio River. It does not include locations such as Steubenville and East Palestine, Ohio, or Beaver Falls and Pittsburgh, Pennsylvania. This publication does include certain manufacturers which have their roots in East Liverpool and subsequently moved to other areas. For example, the Sebring Pottery Company began operations at East Liverpool in 1887 prior to establishing, in 1900, the town of Sebring, Ohio, for the manufacture of pottery. It is estimated that the companies included in this publication produced 60% to 70% of the total ceramic production of the United States between 1880 and 1950. A thorough study of the other ceramic producers located in the tri-state area awaits future publications.

A brief general history of the inception, growth, maturation, and decline of East Liverpool's pottery industry precedes the company histories and marks. This perspective allows the user of this guide to place the potteries and marks into a historical framework. Information regarding the types of ceramic products manufactured in the area, marketing outlets and techniques, and the background of local pottery marks also is included.

The main body of the manuscript includes a concise history of each pottery and illustrations of the firm's marks. These histories are skeletal in nature, providing basic information such as name changes, dates, and the types of pottery or porcelain produced. This approach should provide sufficient information to make accurate judgements concerning the identification and dating of artifacts.

Although Edwin Barber's publications and other secondary works were consulted, primary sources comprised the bulk of the research. These primary materials included; newspapers, diaries, company advertisements, ledgers, legal documents, catalogs, trade journals, eyewitness accounts, and various reports of pottery industry organizations. Also contacted for information were contemporary company executives, designers, and employees. The vast majority of the marks were taken from the ware. Most of these artifacts form the collection of the East Liverpool Museum of Ceramics (Ohio Historical Society). Other examples were found in private collections, local potteries, and collections of local historical societies. Additional sources of marks included proofs from original brass

and zinc dyes, company ledgers, advertisements, catalogs, price lists, rubber stamps, sherds, and other museum collections. Dating information for marks was also gleaned from the above sources.

In order to maintain the integrity of detail often lost during drafting or freehand replication of marks, all of the manufacturer's marks have been reproduced photographically. Except for those marks reprinted from Barber (1904), each figure has a centimeter measure with millimeter demarcation. Preference was given to marks photographed from ware, however, when photo clarity suffered, marks from the primary sources listed above were utilized. In these cases, careful attention was directed to ascertaining that the production mark and the printed mark were the same die.

Use of the Catalog

The pottery manufacturers are listed alphabetically. In instances where more than one partnership or corporation is noted in the heading, the key individual was used to determine alphabetical placement. For example, William Flentke was technically a member of three different firms operating in the same location. Because of the consistent involvement of Flentke, all three separate entities are grouped together under Flentke. Appendix E is a guide to company names and the designations applied to individual buildings used in the text. This appendix should help clarify much of the confusion presently existing about the potteries of East Liverpool.

Whenever possible, marks are grouped chronologically and by associated motifs. Figure captions convey information in the following sequence: the type of ware on which the mark appears, date(s) when the mark was used on ware, and the origin of the mark pictured in the figure. Additional information and data are included, when pertinent, following these three basic divisions. Figure 7a provides the following example: ironstone dinnerware (type of ware mark used on), 1875–1882 (date mark used), ware (source of mark). The sources of the various marks are as follows: ware (artifact), company stamp (provided by manufacturer), Quality Stamp Company and Modern Stamp Company (companies that produced the rubber stamps), company ledger, catalog, etc. (manuscript collection), and Barber (mark photographed from this publication).

In order to facilitate the use of the catalog, an index to the pottery marks based on motifs (Appendix F) is included. An index of individuals names, company names, and the names given to pottery buildings appear at the end of the publication. Other appendices include decorators marks (Appendix A), double and over stamps (Appendix B), trademarks erroneously published as back stamps (Appendix C), and manufacturers for which marks have not been located (Appendix D).

History of the East Liverpool Ceramic Industry

East Liverpool, Ohio, was the nation's largest and most important producer of ceramic table and toilet wares during the late 19th and early 20th centuries. During this period, East Liverpool, known as the "Crockery City," surpassed Trenton, New Jersey, in terms of such production and came to dominate the American pottery industry. In 1887 East Liverpool boasted 21 general ware potteries which employed 2,558 operatives. By 1923 the number of firms had decreased to 17 but the number of employees had jumped to 7,000. These local potteries operated 270 kilns and produced ceramic products valued at $25,000,000. The key to the success of the East Liverpool pottery industry was rooted in broad economic factors such as natural resources, a strategic geographic location, favorable markets, and available transportation facilities. However, the pioneering efforts of early potters and the capable leadership of later entrepreneurs were also important factors in the transformation of the small river town into the "Crockery City" (State Report-

1877 as cited in Howe 1889: 460; Finance and Industry 1923: 7).

East Liverpool, located on the Ohio River 40 miles northwest of Pittsburgh, Pennsylvania, and 52 miles north of Wheeling, West Virginia, was founded in 1799 by Thomas Fawcett. During its early years, St. Clair (the town's official name even though it was called Fawcettstown by its residents) grew slowly. By 1816, the town, renamed Liverpool, consisted of only a few dwellings, a grist mill, and a tavern which doubled as a ferry house. Although additional lots were laid out, the town failed to prosper as major land transportation routes by-passed Liverpool in favor of nearby Wellsville. In effect, this predicament cut the struggling community off from trade and commerce. By 1823 the population consisted of only six families and two bachelors. A resident of the town described Liverpool in 1826 as ". . . perhaps the most forlorn of any located on the Ohio River" (Mack 1879: 173–75; Smith 1888: 3–21).

During the 1830s, the town started to awaken from its sluggish beginnings. Incorporated as East Liverpool in 1834, it began to develop as a local commercial center for the county's agricultural products. Boat building enterprises also boosted the economy. It was the manufacture of pottery, however, that became the cornerstone of East Liverpool's growth and development. As towns sprang up along the Ohio River during the early decades of the 19th century, the increasing population of these settlements offered a ready market for locally manufactured products. A growing need for utilitarian household wares and storage vessels provided the stimulus for the production of earthenwares in the upper Ohio Valley (Mack 1879: 175, 176; Smith 1888: 27–43; Wade 1959: 193–95).

If favorable markets provided the stimulus for pottery production, then the rich clay deposits in the area and the skills of English potters made it a reality. James Bennett, born in Newhall, Burton-on-Trent, South Derbyshire, England, established East Liverpool's first pottery in 1839. Bennett fired his first kiln of earthenware in 1840. In 1841 he encouraged his three brothers, still living in England, to join him in East Liverpool. Upon their arrival, the Bennett Brothers Pottery produced the mottled brown-glazed "Rockingham" ware in addition to yellow earthenware. "Bennett's Liverpool Ware" was advertised as early as 1841 in Pittsburgh and reached crockery merchants in Cleveland, Cincinnati, Louisville, and St. Louis. Prior to this local potteries generally served only local needs. The commercial nature of Bennett's single-kiln pottery and subsequent East Liverpool potteries, combined with the technical skill and methods of these English potters assured the success and development of the emerging pottery industry (Pioneer 1876; Barber 1893, reprint ed. 1976: 194–95).

In 1844 George Garner, a thrower at the Bennett pottery, wrote to his family and friends in England that:

> East Liverpool is full of clay and coal, and contains about 700 inhabitants, lying on the Ohio River, 45 miles from Pittsburgh. It lies well for shipping to Cincinnati, also New Orleans, and many other markets . . . . I find there are markets open to receive every cup of ware that is made. . . . It is impossible for you to starve. . . . Provisions are very cheap. . . . (Manuscript collection of the East Liverpool Historical Society housed at the Ohio Historical Society's East Liverpool Museum of Ceramics, hereafter cited as Mss. ELMC, Garner letter 1844).

Throughout the decades preceding the Civil War many English potters heeded this or similar opinions and arrived in the fledgling pottery town. Pioneer potters such as Benjamin Harker, Sr., John Goodwin, James Salt, William Brunt, Sr., Jabez Vodrey, Frederick Mear, and Thomas Croxall established small potteries producing yellow ware and Rockingham vessels from local clays. In 1849 Jabez Vodrey stated that, "hardly a week passes without some new arrival of potters. . . ." As a group these English potters possessed the skill and technical knowledge necessary to establish the pottery industry in East Liverpool. They adapted their methods, tools, timehonored traditions, and simple machinery to

produce a quality ceramic ware from local clays. By the end of 1850, East Liverpool was seen as a ". . . very agreeable and prosperous town. . . ." The same visitor also commented on the new potteries that had been recently built and the fact that ". . . a large number of elegant brick and frame buildings for dwellings and stores have been erected within the last year." The "forlorn" hamlet was beginning to grow and develop (Pioneer 1876; United States Census 1850, 1860; Vodrey Diary 11 November 1849; Pittsburgh Morning Post 13 November 1850).

By 1853 East Liverpool could boast of 11 potteries which employed 387 operatives and produced $175,000 worth of earthenwares per year. Many of these potteries were small make-shift affairs and most only supported the operation of a single kiln. The largest pottery in East Liverpool at the time was that of Woodward, Blakeley and Company. Their "Phoenix Pottery" consisted of five large buildings (three brick), three kilns and employed about 40 workers (Wellsville Patriot, hereafter cited as WP 3 September 1850, 24 February 1852, 11 July 1854).

The developing pottery industry received a significant boost with the 1852 completion of the Cleveland and Pittsburgh Railroad to Wellsville and with an extension through East Liverpool completed four years later. No longer restricted to river transportation routes, the railroad provided access to new markets for local potteries. As early as 1857, East Liverpool pottery manufacturers linked themselves with nation-wide rail connections and distributed "Ohio Liverpool ware, known as Rockingham and Yellow ware" to wholesalers in New Orleans and Chicago. During the next 10 years (1857–1867), despite the disruptive effects of a nation-wide economic panic and the Civil War, the local industry continued to expand (WP 17 February 1852, 23 September 1856; Mss. ELMC, Catalog—Abbey and Co. 1857; WP, 23 December 1862, 10 June 1862, 18 August 1863).

Except for the short-lived whiteware production of William Bloor (1861–1862) and various experiments by other potters, East Liverpool manufacturers confined themselves to Rockingham and yellow ware prior to 1872. These earthenwares, produced from local clays, were in great demand throughout the south, midwest, and western areas of the country. Indeed, several local potteries made yellow ware and Rockingham well into the 20th century. However, it was during the 1880–1930 period, when most East Liverpool potteries produced whitewares, that the local industry enjoyed its greatest prosperity (Thomas diary 28 March 1861; WP 30 April 1861, 12 November 1850; Goodwin Cup 1846; Mss. ELMC, McNicol catalog 1927, C.C. Thompson Pottery Company price list 1914).

Unlike the natural buff-colored clay abundant in the area of East Liverpool, many of the raw materials necessary to produce whiteware did not exist in the upper Ohio Valley. The principal ingredients, kaolin or china clay and ball clay, and some of the flint and feldspar, were imported from domestic sources in Missouri, Texas, and Georgia or from England. Despite the absence of indigenous raw materials, the existence of a skilled labor force, well established plants, an abundant fuel supply, a strong protective tariff, and continued access to major established markets made the transition to whiteware not only feasible but profitable as well.

During the late 19th and early 20th centuries, the pottery industry experienced a period of unprecedented growth and expansion. In 1877 twenty-three firms producing pottery were located in East Liverpool; 9 of these produced whiteware, 11 Rockingham and yellow ware, 1 manufactured tile, and 2 produced door and furniture knobs. The products of these firms reached far beyond the industry's traditional markets in the south and midwest to areas such as Boston and New York in the East and the entire West. This period also marks the emergence of more sophisticated technology, as evidenced by mechanical improvements, and the use of mass production

methods in the pottery industry. Complex machinery, such as blungers, filter presses, and jiggers, combined with the use of natural gas and steam power (and later electricity), allowed potters to standardize and accelerate production. As early as 1877, Knowles, Taylor and Knowles used natural gas to fire its kilns. By the late 1870s, support industries had sprung up to supply and prepare raw materials, to design and decorate ware, to manufacture tools, equipment and machinery, and to produce barrels, for shipping. By 1895 East Liverpool had surpassed Trenton as the nation's leading producer of dinner and toilet wares. The industry completely dominated the city of East Liverpool, employing almost 90% of the industrial wage earners. This prosperity was reflected in the growth of the city. Population figures provide a convenient index of this growth: a population of 2,105 persons in 1870 soared to more than 20,000 by 1910 (East Liverpool Tribune, hereafter cited as ELT 25 August 1877, 7 October 1876, 18 August 1883, 18 August 1877, 4 April 1876; WP 22 April 1862; State of Ohio, Bureau of Labor Statistics, 1895: 31–32; McCord 1905: 160–179; U.S. Census 1870, 1910; U.S. Government Report, "Pottery Industry" 1915).

During the first quarter of the 20th century, the industry continued to prosper, with an annual production valued at $25,000,000 by 1923. The methods employed by manufacturers to market and distribute their goods were revamped during this era. Tablewares were made available through mail order catalogs and wholesale distributors. Housewives were offered dinnerware as giveaways and premiums with the purchases of cereal, movie tickets, flour, newspaper subscriptions, and other products being promoted by "free dinnerware." Punch card schemes, offered by several East Liverpool potteries, were also used. Department stores and other retail outlets stocked and sold "china," further expanding the market (Finance and Industry, 1923: 7; McKee 1966: 52–55; Mss. ELMC, West End Pottery Company catalog, circa

1920, Harker Pottery Company catalog, circa 1918; Sears, Roebuck and Company catalog 1902.)

By 1930, East Liverpool had reached its zenith. At this time, over 7,000 people were employed in area potteries. During the previous 20 years, however, the "Crockery City" had become the nucleus of a district rather than an actual production center as potteries moved to surrounding areas. Ironically, the city's geographic location, so important in its development, now betrayed it and contributed toward the decline. The Ohio River and the adjacent hills formed permanent geographical barriers to expansion. With land values high, railroad sidings difficult to obtain, and single level factory designs impractical because of limited land, many prominent firms left East Liverpool. The Sebrings moved the French China Company and the Sebring Pottery Company to the new town bearing their name in 1901. In 1912 the management of the French China Company stated that they left East Liverpool in order to build a new modern plant and they were ". . . not content to follow the antiquated methods of a past generation. . . ." The firm of Taylor, Lee and Smith built a pottery in Chester, West Virginia, just across the river from East Liverpool. Other firms, such as the Edwin M. Knowles China Company and the Harker Pottery Company, made the same move at later dates. During this period potteries were also started in nearby Newell, West Virginia, Wellsville, and Salineville, Ohio (see individual histories for dates and documentation). By 1940 only six major dinnerware potteries and a handful of other ceramic manufacturers remained active in the immediate area (Finance and Industry 1923: 7; Mss. ELMC, French China Company catalog 1912).

The reasons for the decline in the number of companies engaged in the ceramic industry are many and these causes vary from company to company. Some firms failed because of mismanagement or because they were unable to compete with other local potteries. As previously noted, many firms moved out of East Liverpool, while others were unable to afford the high cost of new and efficient innovations, such as the tunnel kiln. In addition, new competing products, such as plastic and pyrex also contributed toward the industry's problem. During the 1930s, increased foreign competition, especially from Japan, coupled with lower protective tariffs, presented serious obstacles. These threatening economic factors interacted with the Great Depression of the 1930s to force many potteries to suspend operations. A severe blow to the area's economy occurred when the American Chinaware Corporation, a 1929 consolidation of eight local pottery corporations, went into receivership in 1931. By 1935 the decline in the number of potteries had prompted a local journalist to lament that where the potteries once stood ". . . one now finds filling stations, vacant lots, tumbledown walls and kilns, or gray old potteries . . . their antiquated upright kilns and rusting smoke stacks seeming almost like tombstones in an industrial graveyard." (East Liverpool News 10 May 1935, 29 March 1935; Pittsburgh Sunday Sun-Telegraph 17 April 1938; Ceramic Industry 1938: 35; Mss. ELMC, American Chinaware Corporation-records of formation 1929, bankruptcy claim #23656 1931).

The middle decades of the 20th century (1930–1960) witnessed domination of the local industry by the few firms (Homer Laughlin China Company, Edwin M. Knowles China Company, Harker Pottery Company, Taylor, Smith and Taylor, Hall China Company, Sterling China Company) that managed to survive the perils of the previous quarter century. These firms had employed the latest technologies, adopted techniques and methods of effective business and financial management, developed unique products, or they were able to follow or initiate trends and innovations within the American dinnerware industry. With most of the local competition eliminated, these firms, and other area potteries in Sebring, Salem, and East Palestine, Ohio, turned out a wide variety of ceramic products for the American household. Bright and pastel solid-color glazes and a more informal shape in the dinnerware lines were especially popular during much of this period. Other products which came into popular usage included the oven-to-table and refrigerator-to-table lines.

Another aspect of this period was the resurgence and proliferation of small, single-operator-type potteries and decorating shops. It was as though the local industry had come full circle from the fledgling potteries of a century before to these relatively small-scale operations. Just as their pioneer predecessors had, these firms filled a production void and provided products and services for demanding markets. In general, they produced specialty items and decorated blanks manufactured by other local potteries (see Appendix A).

Despite the absence of many actual manufacturers within East Liverpool's city limits during the past half century, the city has retained its reputation as the center of the American pottery industry. Because of the important role East Liverpool played in the development of the industry, local firms throughout the 20th century have continued to use East Liverpool as their mailing address and in their advertisements.

East Liverpool Ceramic Products

The potteries of East Liverpool range in size from Emanuel Booth's single-kiln earthenware washboard factory of 1876, to the Homer Laughlin China Company which operated five plants with a capacity of 181 kilns in 1929. (ELT 19 August 1876; Mss. ELMC, company catalog 1929). The ceramic products of East Liverpool are as diverse as their producers, varying from common brick, sewer pipe, and electrical porcelain to art pottery and fine bone china. Although common utilitarian crockery, and later dinnerware, were the mainstays of East Liverpool's ceramic production, local potteries produced virtually every type of ceramic product in use during the 19th and 20th centuries.

Throughout its history, "Crockery City"

potters, as well as other manufacturers, have produced a wide variety of ceramic wares referred to by a number of industry and domestic names. Pottery terminology, as it applies to the types and shapes of ware, can be very confusing, if not totally misleading. Without delving into a technical discussion of body or paste types, a brief explanation of these terms will provide a framework for understanding references in this text.

The first products of East Liverpool's potteries were yellow ware and Rockingham. Both of these earthenware types were formed from clays indigenous to the upper Ohio Valley. Once fired, these clays appeared as a buff to a yellow color. Yellow ware was then covered with a clear lead-based glaze, whereas Rockingham is a mottled brown-glazed yellow ware. Often mistakenly referred to as "Bennington" ware, Rockingham wares vary in glaze color from a rich tan to a dark brown in a variety of swirled or mottled designs, Without a manufacturers' mark, positive identification of Rockingham is impossible. Both Rockingham and yellow ware were grouped under the term "Liverpool" ware and the trade name "Queensware," during the mid-19th century. Occasionally, yellow ware was called "cane-colored" ware. Very little stoneware was produced in East Liverpool.

Whiteware is a generic term which encompasses any type of pottery or porcelain that is white, or nearly white, in color. With the exception of majolica and other colored glazes such as Fiesta and Vistosa, a clear glaze normally is used to allow the color of the clay to show through. Under the heading of whiteware there are a variety of actual types as well as a variety of trade names.

The first whiteware products produced in East Liverpool were porcelains. Between 1861 and 1862, William Bloor manufactured Parian and a "double-thick" hotel china. Parian is porcelain which is left unglazed in order to resemble the pure white parian marble after which it is named. Most hotel china is also porcelain, but it is covered with a clear glaze. The post-World War I hotel chinas and some of the oven wares produced during the 20th century by such firms as the Hall China Company are also porcelain products. The two other types of porcelains produced in East Liverpool were Belleek china and Lotus ware. Belleek has an ivory-color body with a pronounced translucency. Lotus ware is not a true porcelain but bone china with a pure white body that is also translucent. Both were covered with a clear glaze. In comparison to other whiteware products, very little porcelain was made in East Liverpool.

The largest class of whitewares produced in East Liverpool fall under the general category of white earthenwares. This production began in 1872 at the pottery of Knowles, Taylor, and Knowles. Essentially, these products were a mixture of ball and china clay, flint, and feldspar, and were known by a variety of trade names such as "ironstone china," "white granite," "pearl china," "granite ware," "flint ware," "porcelain granite," "stone china," "opaque porcelain," "pearl white," "pearl granite," and "opaque china." All of these terms were used by the trade indiscriminately to indicate a grade or type of white earthenware. Despite the claim to "china" or "porcelain," the bodies are all porous and therefore not porcelain (china) at all. The coloration of "Crockery City" ironstone varies from a creamy-white to a bluish-white or grayish tint.

Two other types of whitewares were also produced in East Liverpool district potteries. Majolica ware, produced by two George Morley firms, is also white earthenware, but decorated with very colorful glazes which almost entirely cover the body. The lowest quality whiteware is called c.c. ware (common-clay or cream-colored); c.c. ware is composed of the same basic ingredient as ironstone, but is not as finely processed as the latter. The result is a yellowish or light buff-colored ware. At least one local pottery (Cartwright Brothers) advertised semi-granite wares which we suspect were actually a c.c. type. The ironstone and c.c. classes of white earthenware formed the mainstay of East Liverpool's production during the late nineteenth century.

Another type of whiteware product made at East Liverpool is known as "semi-porcelain" or "semi-vitreous porcelain." Introduced around 1890 in East Liverpool, this ware was produced by the use of more refined clays, in somewhat different proportions than ironstone, and the firing of the body at a higher temperature in an attempt to promote vitrification. As a result, the ware generally can be made thinner than ironstone and approaches the quality of china or porcelain; however, technically it is earthenware. Semi-porcelain is opaque and porous. The term semi-vitreous is actually a misnomer because a ceramic body is either vitreous or it is not. Local potters used these trade names to best advantage when marketing their products throughout the 20th century.

Just as potters developed a variety of trade names for their products which differed from what they actually were, the names used to identify shapes also varied considerably according to their own distinctive system. Generally, shape terminology is based on function rather than form and trade names differ from common names. Table 1 is taken from a 1920 catalog of the Homer Laughlin China Company and should clarify most questions or inconsistencies in determining a shape (Mss. ELMC, Company catalog 1920).

The following terminology is used in this volume to identify general ware types. Toilet ware is considered to be decorated domestic items of the type listed under that title in Table 1. Sanitary wares include open soap dishes, industrial type chamber pots, urinals, bed pans and the like. Dinnerware encompasses only traditional forms for the consumption of food, such as plates, cups and saucers, and salad bowls. Tableware includes dinnerware as well as serving pieces such as tea and coffee pots and pitchers. Oven and refrigerator wares are self-explanatory. Flatware refers to plates, saucers, platters and the like, whereas holloware means cups, pitchers, bowls and so forth.

TABLE 1

COMMON AND TRADE SHAPE NAMES

Dinnerware

Trade Names	Common Names
Plates, 4 inch	Bread and butter plates
Plates, 5 inch	Pie plates
Plates, 6 inch	Breakfast plates
Plates, 7 inch	Dinner plates
Plates, 8 inch	Large dinner plates
Plates, 7 inch deep	Soup plates with rim
Coupe Soups	Soup plates without rim
Bakers	Oval vegetable dishes, uncovered
Nappies	Round vegetable dishes, uncovered
Covered Dishes	Oval vegetable dishes, covered
Casseroles	Round vegetable dishes, covered
Dishes	Oval meat dishes or platters
Fruits	Sauce or dessert dishes
Jugs	Pitchers
Sauce boats	Gravy boats

Toilet Ware

Ewer	Large water pitcher
Mouth ewer	Small hot water pitcher
Basin	Wash bowl
Brush vase	Tooth brush holder
Combinet	Slop jar with wire bail
Cuspidore	Uncovered, unhandled slop jar
Spittoon	Cuspidor

East Liverpool Pottery Marks

East Liverpool pottery marks have an interesting history of their own. The evolution of these marks, the various genres and motifs of the marks, and the use of these marks are fascinating, if somewhat elusive, studies. During the mid-19th century, only a handful of local potteries marked their yellow ware and Rockingham products. The firms that did mark their wares, such as Harker and Goodwin (see also Bennett, Bloor, Harrison), included the mark in the mold or impressed the mark into the body of the piece. However, this was the exception rather than the rule; most East Liverpool potteries did not employ a mark (at least none has surfaced to date for these firms). The exact reason for this is unknown, but it probably occurred because many of the wares were considered to be common utilitarian housewares. Even when "Crockery City" manufacturers began turning out white ironstone in large quantities during the 1870s, much of it was left unmarked.

Throughout the second half of the 19th century, East Liverpool, and other American pottery centers as well, had to confront and attempt to overcome a long standing preference by American consumers for pottery made in England. Even though American products, for the most part, were equal in quality to British imports, there existed a noticeable lack of acceptance. In reaction to this prejudice, a great deal of ironstone was either left unmarked or marked with an English-type mark in order to deceive consumers. The practice of using familiar British symbols such as the lion and unicorn in combination with a coat of arms, a heraldic escutcheon, or a shield was prevalent throughout the late 1880s. Occasionally the diamond-shaped registry mark or the familiar garter-shaped mark also appeared on American pottery. As late as 1894, John Maddock and Sons of England advertised its pottery mark on the cover of its price list with the following: "This stamp is being imitated. It is easier to imitate the stamp than the goods" (Barber 1904:44; Mss. ELMC, Company price list 1894). The subterfuge of imitating foreign trademarks was not unique to American potteries in the 19th century. During the 18th century, it was not uncommon for Chinese marks to be imitated by English potteries.

East Liverpool potteries faced stiff competition from English producers throughout the late 19th and early 20th centuries. However, American manufacturers gained continually in prestige and acceptance as time went on. High protective tariffs and lower railroad rates throughout much of this period helped domestic potteries compete on a favorable basis with British imports. The Centennial celebration of 1876 and the Chicago World's Fair in 1893 also helped native potteries gain recognition in the battle for American markets. These, along with other lesser exhibits of the period, provided a showcase in which ceramics could be compared. At least two East Liverpool firms, Brunt, Bloor, Martin and Company and the Laughlin Brothers, won high awards at the Centennial for their whiteware. Knowles, Taylor and Knowles won a premium for Lotus Ware in 1893. American ironstone was beginning to be accepted as equal to English imports. Pottery marks also reflected, or perhaps encouraged, this change (ELT 30 September 1876).

In 1877 an East Liverpool firm, the Laughlin Brothers Pottery Company, introduced a pottery mark (Figure 111) which blatantly declared American pottery superior to English wares. The mark depicted the American eagle triumphant over a prostrate British lion (ELT 25 August 1877). The symbolism was unmistakeable. Even though several Trenton potteries had used marks which stated the place of manufacture prior to the appearance of the Laughlin Brothers mark, the challenge to

British domination in the industry had not before been so dramatically issued. Other East Liverpool potteries soon followed Laughlin's lead. In 1878 Knowles, Taylor and Knowles (Figure 1) patented its first pottery mark, an American bison which clearly signified American chauvinism. The George S. Harker Pottery Company began using crossed American flags in its mark as early as 1879 (Mss. ELMC, United States Patent #5503 15 January 1878). The emergence of these characteristically American marks did not bring the use of spurious English marks to an end; many East Liverpool potteries continued to use them throughout the late 19th century. Many other pottery marks used by domestic manufac-

FIGURE 1. Worker at the Knowles, Taylor and Knowles pottery in 1901 applying a pottery mark to a piece of ware. Photo courtesy of the Ohio Historical Society.

turers during the period 1875 to about 1910 tended to be either very elaborate, employing a myriad of shapes and designs, or very simply using the name of a particular shape in script or block letters. The pottery marks dating from 1910 to the present day are, as a rule, either very plain and straightforward, or utilize a highly stylized motif. Most contemporary marks are less artistic than their predecessors and illustrate no real attempt at embellishment. Pottery marks are a dependable means by which ceramics may be identified. However, even these manufacturers marks can be misleading or blatant forgeries. A piece of Lotus Ware recently examined at the East Liverpool Museum of Ceramics was marked with the Laughlin's Lion/Eagle (Figure 111) mark. The Laughlin pottery never produced Lotus Ware (see Knowles, Taylor and Knowles) but it would have been very easy for a worker to smuggle a piece out of the plant and give it to his friend working up the street at Laughlin's pottery. Despite this anomaly, pottery marks remain the single most valuable tool that we have for the identification of pottery and porcelain.

ACME CRAFTWARE, INC. (Figure 2)   1941–1970

   Acme Craftware was founded in 1941 by Roland and Mary Bryer Leonard as a retail and wholesale distributor of pottery in Wellsville, Ohio. Shortly after its inception, the firm began decorating ware and eventually started manufacturing high-grade pottery. On 12 July 1944, the firm, which by now also included John and Julia Mountford, Albert Vandyne, and John and Eva Bryer, was incorporated under the name of Acme Craftware Incorporated. The corporation produced artware, novelties, and accessory pieces such as serving dishes, salts and peppers, ewers, ashtrays, and vases. The company's "Weeping Gold" pattern was especially popular. The State of Ohio purchased the Acme Craftware pottery on 3 December, 1969, in order to clear land for a new highway; production was halted soon after that (Roland Leonard 1978, pers. comm.; Mss. ELMC, Company catalog n.d.).

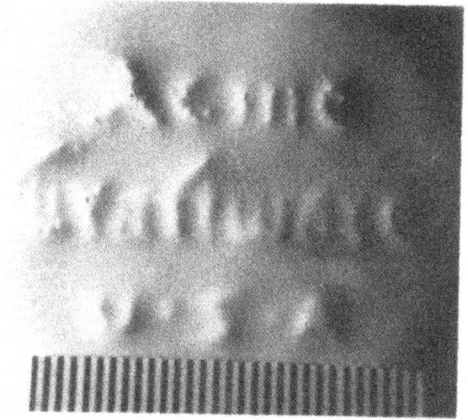 

                                        a   b

FIGURE 2. Acme Craftware, Inc.: a. semi-vitreous novelty artware, 1944–1970, ware, raised; b. semi-vitreous novelty artware, 1944–1970, ware.

AMERICAN CHINAWARE CORPORATION (Figure 3)   1929–1931

   In 1929 eight pottery firms joined to form the American Chinaware Corporation. The merger was an attempt to revitalize the slumping American dinnerware industry. Total assets of these corporations, which included the Carrollton Pottery Company; the E.H. Sebring China Company; Knowles, Taylor and Knowles; the Morgan-Bellek China Company; National China Company; Pope-Gosser China Company; Sebring Manufacturing Corporation; and the Smith-Phillips China Company, totaled almost two million dollars (Mss. ELMC, records of formation 1929). The members of the American Chinaware Corporation represented some of the largest and most prestigious potteries in the nation. The merger, however, proved to be ill-advised, and in 1931 the American Chinaware Corporation was placed in receivership and its component companies ceased to operate (Mss. ELMC, Bankruptcy Claim #23656, 1931). The failure of this corporation was a severe blow to the American pottery industry and to the economy of the East Liverpool pottery district.

FIGURE 3. American Chinaware Corporation: a. semi-vitreous dinnerware, 1929–1931, ware; b. semi-vitreous dinnerware, 1929–1931, ware; c. semi-vitreous dinnerware, 1929–1931, ware.

JAMES H. BAUM (Figure 4)   1888–1896

In 1883 James Baum leased the former decorating shop of George Humrickhouse and began an independent pottery decorating company. Baum, a Harvard graduate, initially prospered in his new establishment. The local newspaper reported in October 1883 that Baum had just introduced two new English patterns and was "... making improvements to increase capacity. . . ." By 1884, however, Thomas Haden had taken over the decorating shop. Research has not revealed any marks used by Baum during this period (ELT 4 August 1883, 27 October 1883; Vodrey 1945: 287).

James Baum disappears from the written record until 1888 when he purchased the "School House Pottery" in Wellsville, Ohio where he produced cream-colored and white ironstone dinnerware. Encouraged perhaps by the success of Trenton manufacturers during the late 1880s and early 1890s, Baum converted his plant to the production of sanitary ware. According to available sources, depressed business conditions and a lack of financial support forced the firm to cease operations in 1896 (McCord 1905: 174).

a

b

FIGURE 4. James H. Baum: a. ironstone dinnerware, 1888–1896, ware; b. ironstone tableware, 1888–1896, ware.

JAMES BENNETT (Figure 5a)   1839–1841
BENNETT BROTHERS (Figure 5b)   1841–1844

James Bennett, born in Newhall, Burton-on-Trent, South Derbyshire, England established East Liverpool's first pottery in 1839. Prior to his arrival in East Liverpool, Bennett worked at American potteries in Jersey City, New Jersey, and Troy, Indiana. Upon discovering suitable deposits of coal and clay near the small river town of East Liverpool, he built a pottery to manufacture yellow earthenwares. Bennett's first kiln of yellow ware was fired in 1840 (Pioneer 1876; Barber 1893, reprint ed. 1976: 192–96; Mss. ELMC, Bennett family information n.d.).

Bennett's brothers, Edwin, Daniel, and William, arrived from England in 1841, thus initiating an immigration of skilled Staffordshire potters to the Upper Ohio Valley which continued for generations. James' brothers and other skilled potters helped improve the quality of Bennett's Rockingham and yellow ware. In 1845, at the fifteenth annual Franklin Institute exhibit, the Bennetts won an award for their Rockingham. The society's bulletin stated that ". . . the jugs, mugs, and spittoons are decidedly better than the English Rockingham ware . . ." (As quoted by Stefano 1976: 24).

In 1844 the Bennett Brothers left East Liverpool to establish a pottery in Pittsburgh. Edwin Bennett (joined briefly by William) later founded a pottery in Baltimore, Maryland, which achieved national prominence during the second half of the 19th century. Even though the Bennetts did not remain in Ohio, their pottery was the beginning of a prominent industry in East Liverpool. (Mss. ELMC, Bennett family information n.d.; Pioneer 1876; Barber 1893, Reprint ed. 1976: 143, 192–96).

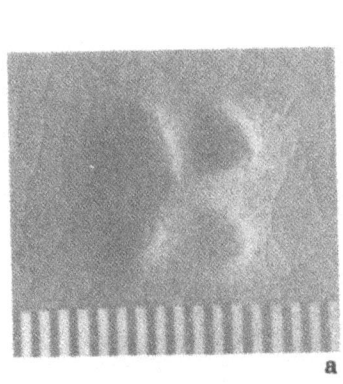
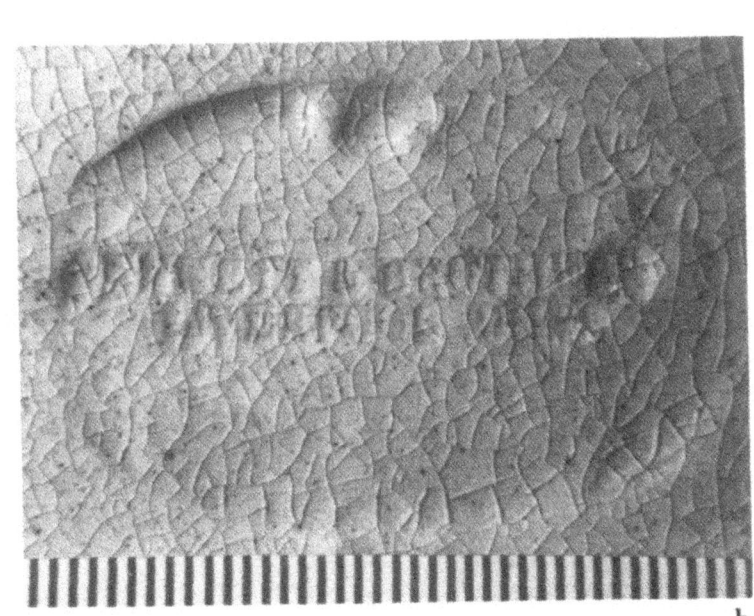

FIGURE 5. James Bennett/Bennett Brothers: a. yellow ware cuspidor, ca. 1843, ware, impressed, attributed by Thorn (1947: 118); b. yellow ware platter, 1841–1844, ware, impressed, reads "BENNETT & BROTHERS/LIVERPOOL OHIO."

WILLIAM BLOOR (Figure 6)   1860–1862

William Bloor established the first white dinnerware potteries in Trenton, New Jersey (1856), and East Liverpool (1861). Bloor, a skilled English potter, operated a yellow ware and Rockingham pottery in East Liverpool with his friend William Brunt in late 1849. In 1855 he moved to Trenton and joined James Taylor and Henry Speeler, two former East Liverpool potters, in the production of ironstone (Bulletin of the American Ceramic Society, hereafter cited as ACS, 1937: 25–31; American Patriot 13 November 1849).

Bloor returned to East Liverpool in 1859 and purchased a section of the "Phoenix Pottery," formerly owned by Woodward, Blakeley and Company and began refitting the works for the production of whiteware. On 28 March 1861, John Thomas, a local English potter, reported in his diary that "Wm. Bloor Sr. Pottery drawd (sic) the first kiln of whiteware." Bloor manufactured "American parian" and "double thick hotel ware" in his new plant. On 28 November 1861, he advertised his "East Liverpool Porcelain Works" in the local newspaper: "Having perfected his experiments, erected extensive works for the purpose, provided abundant material and skillful workmen, he respectfully solicits the attention and patronage of the trade." Chamber sets, tea and dinner sets, pitchers, candlesticks, and curtain tiebacks were all produced. Bloor's products were of a high quality, but he was forced to close his porcelain factory in 1862 because of financial difficulties and a dearth of workmen resulting from the Civil War. Bloor returned to Trenton and established the "Etruria Works" in partnership with J. H. Brewer and Joseph Ott. Returning to East Liverpool in 1870, he eventually began his third local pottery (see Brunt, Bloor, Martin and Company) (WP 14 August 1860; Thomas Diary 28 March 1861; East Liverpool Mercury 28 November 1861; Pioneer 1876).

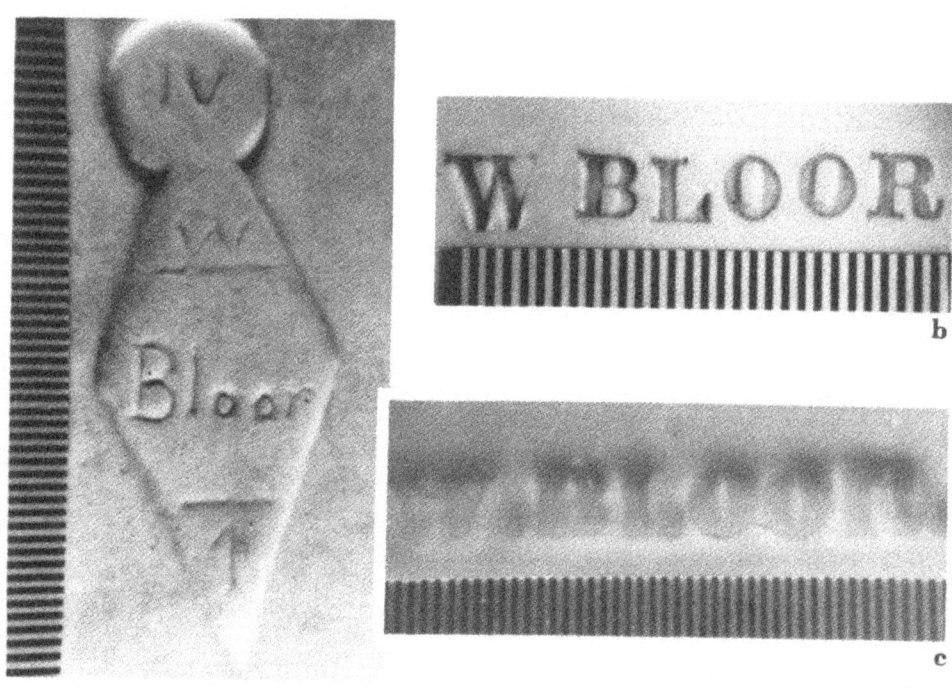

FIGURE 6. William Bloor: a. Parian pitcher, 1861–1862, ware, raised; b. ironstone hotel china plate, 1861–1862, ware, impressed; c. Parian mug, 1861–1862, ware, impressed, variation of Figure 6b.

BRUNT, BLOOR, MARTIN AND COMPANY (Figure 7)   1875–1882

In 1875 William Brunt, Jr., Henry Brunt, George Martin, and the Brunt's brother-in-law William Bloor founded the ''Dresden Pottery Works.'' The company drew its first kiln of whiteware in February 1876. The firm produced an excellent white ironstone and a series of gold decorated wares. Its products included tableware, tea sets, toilet wares, spittoons, toys, and ''double thick hotel ware.'' Brunt, Bloor, Martin and Company won the ''Highest Award and Diploma of Merit'' for their white granite wares at the Centennial Exhibition of 1876 (ELT 4 March 1876; Mss. ELMC, Company Price List ca. 1878).

Eight East Liverpool potteries, in an effort to stop operatives from joining the Knights of Labor, issued an ''Iron-Clad Contract'' in 1882, refusing to allow union sympathizers to work in their factories. Brunt, Bloor, Martin and Company decided not to become involved in the labor struggle and in 1882 sold its plant to a new company, the Potter's Co-operative Company. This new firm was composed of disgruntled potters from a variety of East Liverpool firms that had supported the lock-out (see Potter's Co-operative Company). The closing date of 1892 as noted in Ramsay (1939) and Lehner (1978, 1980) for Brunt, Bloor, Martin and Company is incorrect. Lehner also confuses the manufacturers' marks of these two distinctly separate firms (Mss. ELMC, manuscript 1882; company stock ledger 1882; Calhoun 1922: 105).

FIGURE 7. Brunt, Bloor, Martin and Company: a. ironstone tableware, 1875–1882, ware; b. ironstone dinnerware, 1875–1882, ware.

c

FIGURE 7 continued. c. ironstone teapot, 1875–1882, ware, variation of Figure 7b.

BRUNT ASSOCIATIONS (Figures 8–12)   1848–1911

Several generations of Brunts were associated with potteries in East Liverpool during the second half of the 19th and early 20th centuries, beginning with William Brunt Sr., an English potter. In 1848 he organized a pottery company in partnership with his son-in-law William Bloor. By the summer of 1849, the new firm began the production of yellow ware and Rockingham, but by 1850 it was producing knobs exclusively. In 1853 William Bloor left the firm for the gold fields of California. Three years later (1856) Henry Brunt and William Brunt Jr. joined the firm and it became known as William Brunt and Brothers. William Jr. withdrew in 1859 and Henry Brunt and his sons continued to operate the plant known as the "Riverside Knob Works" (American Patriot 13 November 1849; Pioneer 1876).

By 1876 the company was one of the largest producers of door and furniture knobs in the nation, shipping over three million knobs per year. In 1884 the company added electrical porcelain to its production. George F. Brunt, another of Henry's sons, and his brother-in-law Charles Thompson, operated the electrical section of the plant known as the G.F. Brunt Porcelain Works. The Brunt family ended their interest in the two enterprises in 1910 when they disposed of their holdings to an undetermined buyer. By 1918, the plants were operated by the General Porcelain Company, The knob works and the porcelain company continued to operate until the mid to late 1930s under different ownership (Pioneer 1876; Calhoun 1922: 55; Vodrey 1945: 282; ELMC, Company stationery 1935).

When William Brunt Jr. withdrew from the knob works in 1859, he purchased a section of the former Woodward, Blakeley and Company's "Phoenix" pottery when that firm ceased operations. Brunt began to ready the plant for the production of yellow and Rockingham wares. By October 1860, the Phoenix Pottery was once again in operation. When William Bloor left East Liverpool for Trenton, New Jersey, in late 1862, Brunt purchased his whiteware establishment and converted the plant to the production of Rockingham and yellow ware. With both potteries united into one, Brunt significantly increased his production capacity. However, the Civil War placed a strain on the production of pottery in East Liverpool and in 1865 Brunt sold his original pottery to a firm composed of John Thompson, William Jobling, James Taylor, and John Hardwick. Brunt retained the name "Phoenix Pottery" for his new plant and the new owners of his original plant renamed it the "Lincoln Pottery" (WP 14 August 1860, 3 February 1863; Pioneer 1876).

William Brunt Jr. and Company continued to manufacture Rockingham and yellow ware. A price list dated 1865–1866 advertised pitchers, spittoons, mugs, pie plates, chamber pots, bowls bakers, snuff jars, and butter pots. The pottery prospered and within a few years Brunt employed about 45 workers and produced nearly $50,000 worth of earthenwares per year (Mss. ELMC company price list, 1865–1866; Pioneer 1876).

In 1877 Brunt refitted his entire plant with up-to-date machinery and equipment and converted the operation to the production of white ironstone. He also converted his coal-fired kilns and boilers to natural gas. The following year, Brunt brought his son William, and son-in-law Brad M. Louthan, into the firm which became known as William Brunt Son and Company. The firm incorporated in 1892 as the William Brunt Pottery Company. In 1911 because of careless management, reckless expenditures, and the withdrawal of some of the partners, the once prosperous firm closed. This final Brunt association produced plain and decorated ironstone toilet ware, spittoons, dinner and tea sets, shaving mugs, moustache cups, and toy tea sets. All of the marks presented here are those of the "Phoenix Pottery," (ELT 14 July 1877; Calhoun 1922: 55–57; Mss. ELMC, Company letterhead n.d., Company price list ca. 1888; Proceedings of the Thirty-third Annual Convention of the United States Potters Association 1911: 23; hereafter cited as USPA).

Although William Brunt Jr. operated his own firm, he was also associated with two other potteries. In 1867, in partnership with his brother Henry and H. R. Hill, he organized the firm of Hill, Brunt and Company. This pottery, known as the "Great Western Pottery Works," produced Rockingham and yellow ware until 1874 when it was sold to John Wyllie and Son (Mss. ELMC, business card n.d.; Ramsay 1939: 218). To date, no pottery marks have been located for this firm. Following the sale of the "Great Western" pottery, Brunt became a partner in the firm of Brunt, Bloor, Martin and Company.

FIGURE 8. William Brunt Jr. and Company: a. ironstone tableware, 1877–1878, ware; b. ironstone toilet ware, 1877–1878, ware; c. ironstone dinnerware, 1877–1878, ware; d. ironstone dinnerware, 1877–1878, ware.

FIGURE 9. William Brunt Son and Company: a. ironstone toilet ware, 1878–1892, ware; b. ironstone dinnerware, 1878–1892, ware.

FIGURE 10. William Brunt Pottery Company: a. ironstone dinnerware, 1894, ware; b. semi-vitreous dinnerware, 1892–1911, ware.

FIGURE 10 continued. c. semi-vitreous dinnerware, 1892–1911, ware; d. semi-vitreous dinnerware, 1892–1911, ware.

FIGURE 11. William Brunt Pottery Company: a. ironstone, 1894, Barber (1904: 107); b. semi-vitreous toilet and table ware, 1892–1911, ware.

FIGURE 11 continued. c. semi-vitreous tableware, 1892–1911, ware; d. table and toilet ware, 1877–1911, Barber (1904: 107).

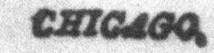

FIGURE 12. William Brunt Associations: a. toilet and table ware, 1877–1911, Barber (1904: 107); b. toilet and table ware, 1877–1911, Barber (1904: 107); c. toilet and table ware, 1877–1911, Barber (1904: 107); d. toilet and table ware, 1877–1911, Barber (1904: 107).

BURFORD BROTHERS (Figures 13–18)   1879–1904

In 1879, Olivar, Robert, and George W. Burford built a pottery for the production of floor and wall tiles. When this venture proved unsuccessful in 1881, they converted the factory to the manufacture of ironstone and c.c. ware. By 1887, they had two kilns in operation and their annual production reached $50,000. Like other East Liverpool potteries, they shipped their products to all sections of the country, but their main markets were in the West and Northwest (Annual Business Review of Columbiana County, Ohio 1887: 26; Calhoun 1922: 114).

By 1890, the c.c. line had been discontinued and the firm only produced ironstone. It offered consumers the typical fare of dinner, tea, and toilet sets as well as spittoons, punch bowls, and accessory pieces. The firm also manufactured a line of hotel ware and ware that it termed "porcelain." The Burford Brothers Pottery Company came to be known for the excellence of its decorative work. Extant pieces indicate a superior product (Mss. ELMC, Company price list 1900).

The Burford Brothers sold their plant to the Standard Pottery Company in 1904 (USPA 1904: 61).

a

b

FIGURE 13. Burford Brothers: a. ironstone dinnerware, ca. 1881, ware, L. missing from "E.L.O." initials; b. ironstone hotel ware and dinnerware accessories, 1881–1904, ware.

FIGURE 13 continued. c. ironstone dinnerware, 1881–1904, ware, see similar mark Figure 13d and Figure 227a; d. ironstone dinnerware, 1881–1904, ware, see similar mark Figure 13c and Figure 227a.

FIGURE 14. Burford Brothers: a. ironstone sanitary ware, ca. 1882, ware.

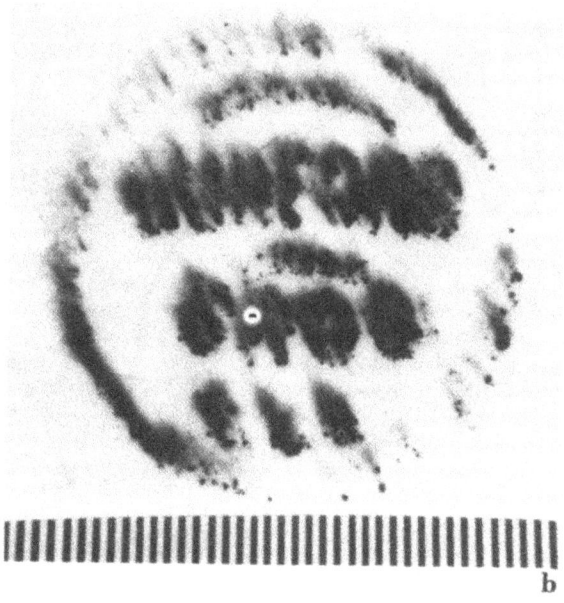

FIGURE 14 continued. b. ironstone dinnerware, 1881–1904, ware; c. ironstone dinnerware accessory, 1881–1904, ware; d. ironstone sanitary ware and kitchenware, 1881–1904, ware.

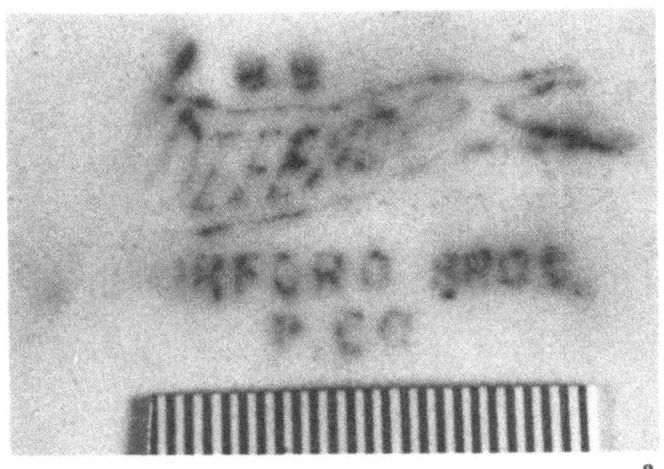

FIGURE 15. Burford Brothers: a. ironstone table and toilet ware, 1881–1904, ware; b. ironstone table and toilet ware, 1881–1904, ware; c. ironstone table and toilet ware, 1881–1904, ware; d. ironstone tableware, 1895–1904, ware, variation—"B.P.C." rather than "B.P. Co."

FIGURE 16. Burford Brothers: a. semi-vitreous dinnerware, ca. 1900, ware; b. semi-vitreous dinnerware, ca. 1900, ware, attributed.

FIGURE 17. Burford Brothers: a. ironstone hotel ware, 1881–1904, ware; b. ironstone hotel ware, 1881–1904, ware, impressed, (photo courtesy of George Miller); c. ironstone toilet ware, ca. 1881–1904, ware; d. ironstone toilet ware, 1881–1904, ware.

a

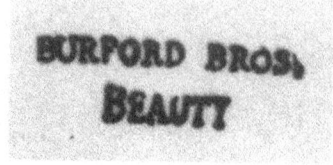

b

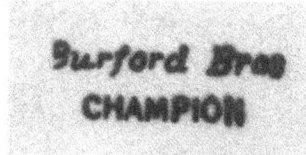

c

d

FIGURE 18. Burford Brothers: a. semi-vitreous ware, ca. 1900, Barber (1904: 116); b. ironstone toilet ware, ca. 1890, Barber (1904: 116); c. ironstone toilet ware, ca. 1890, Barber (1904: 116); d. ironstone dinnerware, ca. 1895, Barber (1904: 116).

MANLEY AND CARTWRIGHT   1864–1880
CARTWRIGHT BROTHERS (Figures 19–23)   1880–1927

Holland Manley, a skilled Staffordshire potter, and William Cartwright purchased the former Webster stoneware pottery in 1864. When the hostilities of the Civil War had ceased, they made extensive improvements to existing facilities and constructed new buildings for the production of Rockingham and yellow wares. The proprietors of the "Industrial Pottery Works" continued to operate the plant successfully and in 1872 Samuel Cartwright, William's brother, purchased an interest in the establishment. At this time, the name was changed to Manley, Cartwright and Company. This partnership continued until 1880 when Manley retired and the name of the firm was changed to the Cartwright Brothers Pottery Company (Pioneer 1876; McCord 1905: 156; Mss. ELMC, Company price list 1872).

In 1887 the firm discontinued the production of Rockingham and yellow ware in favor of semi-granite and cream-colored ware. The firm was incorporated as "The Cartwright Brothers Company" in 1896. At that time, the plant consisted of five ware kilns and two decorating kilns. In 1909 the company added a complete line of "semi-vitreous china" including dinner and hotel wares. The Cartwright Brothers Pottery Company suspended operations in 1927 (Mss. ELMC, Company price list 1914; USPA 1927: 11).

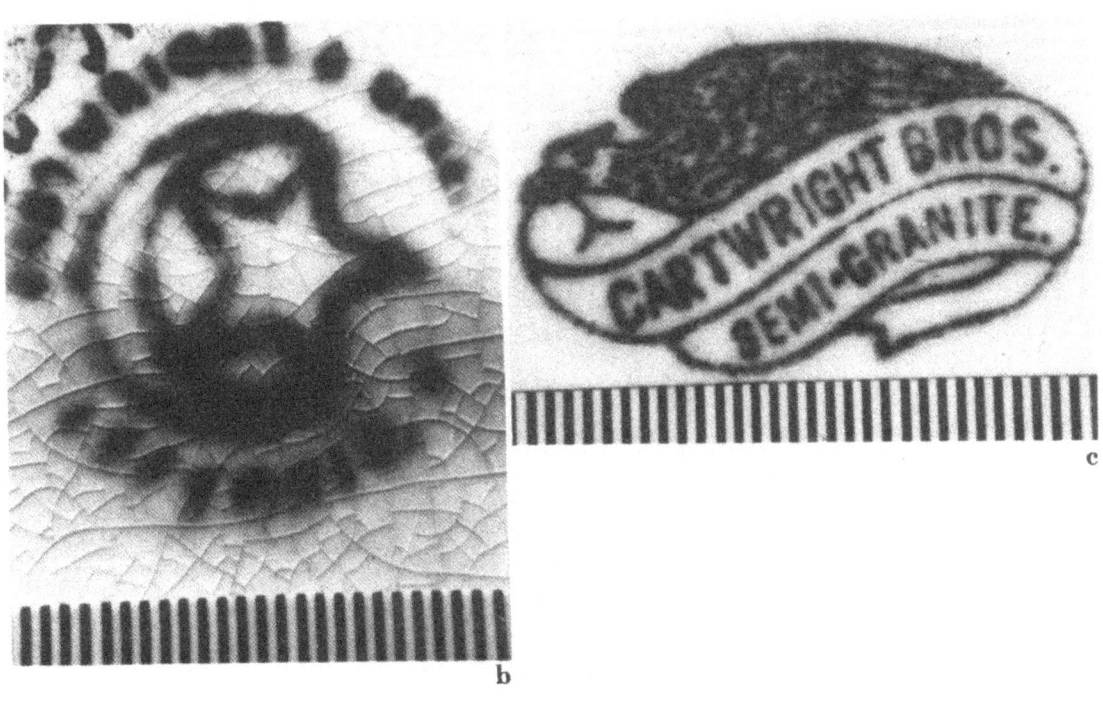

FIGURE 19. Cartwright Brothers: a. cream-colored tableware, 1887–1896, ware; b. ironstone dinnerware, 1887–1896, ware, mark reads "CARTWRIGHT & BROS./LIVERPOOL O."; c. ironstone dinnerware, 1887–ca. 1900, ware.

FIGURE 20. Cartwright Brothers Company: a. ironstone dinnerware, ca. 1905, ware; b. ironstone dinnerware accessory, 1892–ca. 1905, ware; c. ironstone dinnerware, ca. 1905, ware; d. ironstone dinnerware, 1896, ware.

FIGURE 21. Cartwright Brothers Company: a. ironstone tableware, ca. 1888, ware.

b

c

d

FIGURE 21 continued. b. ironstone kitchenware, ca. 1912, ware; c. ironstone dinnerware, 1896–1927, ware; d. ironstone table and toilet ware, 1896–1927, ware, variation of Figure 21c, also "Brooklyn" in ribbon.

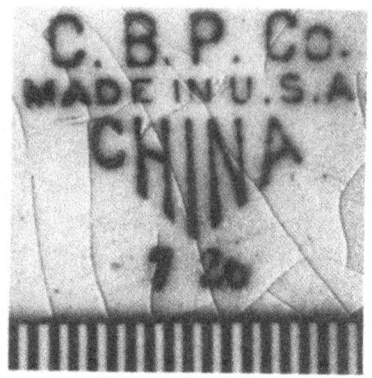

a   b   c

d

FIGURE 22. Cartwright Brothers Company: a. semi-vitreous ware, 1909–1927, Modern Stamp; b. semi-vitreous ware, 1909–1927, Modern Stamp; c. semi-vitreous tableware, ca. 1926, ware, see similar mark "EAST LIVERPOOL POTTERIES COMPANY" (Figure 34c); d. semi-vitreous dinnerware, ca. 1919, ware.

FIGURE 23. Cartwright Brothers: a. semi-vitreous ware, ca. 1918, Modern Stamp; b. ironstone toilet ware, ca. 1900, Barber (1904: 112), shape name.; c. ironstone toilet ware, ca. 1900, Barber (1904: 112), shape name, also "Trent," "Pacific," "Cable" shapes; d. ironstone toilet ware, ca. 1900, Barber (1904: 112).

THE COLONIAL COMPANY (Figures 24–25)   1903–1929

   The Colonial Company grew out of an unsuccessful attempt to merge six potteries into the
East Liverpool Potteries Company. The Colonial Company organized and incorporated in 1903
by Thomas Robinson, Joseph Chetwynd, Christopher Horton and others, operated in the
former Wallace and Chetwynd pottery on River Road. Robinson, an experienced potter who
worked in various East Liverpool plants, had been president and manager of the George C.
Murphy Company which had joined the merger known as the East Liverpool Potteries Company. The Colonial Company manufactured semi-porcelain toilet sets, dinnerware, and ware for
hotels and restaurants. In 1929 the firm halted operations (McCord 1905: 703; Crockery and
Glass Journal 16 December 1915: 132; China and Glass Trade Directory 1927: 39, 44, 46; USPA
1929: 36).

a

b

FIGURE 24. The Colonial Company: a. semi-vitreous ware, 1903–1929, ware; b. semi-vitreous ware, 1903–1929,
ware.

FIGURE 25. The Colonial Company: a. semi-vitreous ware, 1903–1929, ware; b. semi-vitreous ware, 1903–1929, Modern Stamp; c. semi-vitreous ware, 1903–1929, ware.

CONTINENTAL KILNS (Figure 26)   1944–1953 (1957)

Located in Chester, West Virginia, Continental Kilns was formed in 1944 with the former art director of the Edward M. Knowles China Company, Vincent Broomhall, as president. It was Broomhall's intent to manufacture a Belleek-type ware and high quality art ware. Apparently, efforts to achieve this objective were never realized. Marketed under the trade name "China by Vincent," Continental Kilns produced a wide range of china products. These included florists' ware, teaware, artware, kitchen ware, dinnerware, general specialties and premium assortments. On 24 November 1953, Broomhall announced that the pottery was going out of business due to excessive labor costs (East Liverpool Review 28 October 1944; McKee 1967: 33; China and Glass Red Book 1945: 54, 1952: 20; East Liverpool Review 24 November 1953).

Continental Kilns was officially dissolved in 1957 when Metsch Refractories Incorporated of Newell, West Virginia, purchased the works from Broomhall (East Liverpool City Directory, hereafter cited as ELCD, 1958: 71; East Liverpool Review 23 January 1957).

FIGURE 26. Continental Kilns: a. semi-vitreous dinnerware, 1944–1954, ware; b. semi-vitreous dinnerware, 1944–1954, ware; c. semi-vitreous dinnerware, 1944–1954, ware.

CROXALL AND CARTWRIGHT (Figure 27)   1856–1888
CROXALL ASSOCIATIONS   1844–1852/1888–1914

Thomas Croxall, an English potter, was the first of his family to arrive in East Liverpool. That same year (1844), he sent to England for his father and younger brothers, all skilled potters, and, following their arrival, they purchased the former Bennett pottery. During its early years this pottery remained small; in 1848 the pottery consisted of four rooms, one kiln, and employed 10 to 12 operatives. The quality of their ware was considered equal to that of other local potteries. The Croxalls produced yellow ware and Rockingham in this plant until it was destroyed by the flood of 1852 (American Patriot 13 June 1858; McCord 1905: 512).

In 1856 Joseph Cartwright, Thomas and John Croxall, along with Jonathan Kinsey purchased the former "Union Pottery" of Ball and Morris, but within two and a half years Thomas Croxall and Jonathan Kinsey withdrew from the firm. The company became known as Croxall and Cartwright and continued to produce Rockingham and yellow ware (WP 11 March 1856, 12 January 1858, 10 August 1858).

Croxall and Cartwright increased their capacity significantly in 1863 despite the loss of southern markets during the Civil War. In May of that year, the firm acquired the "Mansion" pottery of Salt and Mear in one of the largest real estate transactions in the area. A two-story brick addition to the "Union" works, completed in August, added even more manufacturing capacity. By 1876 Croxall and Cartwright was one of the largest potteries in East Liverpool. At full capacity it employed 100 workers and produced from fifty to sixty thousand dollars worth of ware each year (WP 5 May 1863; Pioneer 1876).

John Croxall acquired Cartwright's interest in the firm in 1888 and brought his two sons, George and Joseph, into the company. The firm was renamed J. W. Croxall and Sons. In 1892 the company produced Rockingham spittoons, bed pans, foot warmers, pitchers, tea pots, bowls, nappies and mugs. Its yellow ware line included butterpots, mugs, bowls, pie plates, pitchers, and covered chambers. In January 1898 the firm was incorporated as the Croxall Pottery Company and continued to operate until 1914 when the pottery was purchased by the American Porcelain Company (McCord 1905: 513; Mss. ELMC, Company price list 1891; Stout 1923: 18).

FIGURE 27. Croxall and Cartwright: a. Rockingham teapot ("Rebecca at the Well" motif), 1870–1888, ware, raised.

DRESDEN POTTERY COMPANY (Figure 28) 1925–1927

The Dresden Pottery Company was incorporated on 10 October 1925. At that time, Harry McNicol, T. A. McNicol, Patrick McNicol, William H. Vodrey, and A. P. McPherson, issued five thousand shares of common stock. This firm began operating the "Dresden Pottery Works" when the Potter's Cooperative Company (see history) disbanded and manufactured semi-vitreous dinnerware, hotel china, and both plain and decorated specialty items. After only two years of operation the Dresden Pottery Company discontinued business (Mss. ELMC, Articles of Incorporation 1925, Company stationery n.d.; USPA 1927: 32).

FIGURE 28. Dresden Pottery Company: a. semi-vitreous dinnerware, 10/1925–1927, ware.

EAST END POTTERY COMPANY (Figures 29a,b-30)   1894–1901/1903–1907
EAST END CHINA COMPANY (Figure 29 c,d)   1908–1909

The East End Pottery Company began in 1894 as a cooperative operation when local potters Edward Owens, Joseph Deekin, Gus Trenle, Sampson Turnbull, and others built a modern two-kiln pottery to produce whiteware. During the 1890s this firm produced underglaze decorated white granite dinner and tea sets. The company's best known product was its "Columbia" line (China, Glass, and Lamps 29 August 1894, 29 January 1897; Calhoun 1922: 131–132).

In 1901 the firm joined the East Liverpool Potteries Company. When this organization partially collapsed in 1903, the East End Pottery Company resumed its former status. During the mid-1890s, the company began manufacturing semi-porcelain toilet and dinnerwares and in 1908 the name of the firm was changed to the East End China Company. At about the same time, Gus Trenle assumed control of the company and in 1909 it became the Trenle China Company (Vodrey 1945: 286; Calhoun 1922: 134; USPA 1908: 14).

a

b

c

d

FIGURE 29. East End Pottery Company: a. semi-vitreous toilet ware, 1894–1901/1903–1907, ware; b. semi-vitreous dinnerware, 1894–1901/1903–1907, ware; c. semi-vitreous dinnerware, 1908–1909, ware, East End China Co.; d. semi-vitreous dinnerware, 1908–1909, ware, East End China Co., see "TRENLE" (Figure 273a, b, c) for similar mark.

a

b

c

d

FIGURE 30. East End Pottery Company: a. ironstone or semi-vitreous toilet ware, 1894–1901/1903–1907, Barber (1904: 115); b. ironstone or semi-vitreous toilet ware, 1894–1901/1903–1907, Barber (1904: 115); c. ironstone or semi-vitreous ware, 1894–1901/1903–1907, Barber (1904: 115); d. ironstone or semi-vitreous ware, 1894–1901/1903–1907, Barber (1904: 115).

EAST LIVERPOOL POTTERY COMPANY (Figures 31–32)   1894–1901

In 1894 John W. and Robert Hall, successful East Liverpool lumber dealers, and Monroe Patterson, an iron founder, combined resources to establish the East Liverpool Pottery Company. This company produced plain and decorated ironstone china until 1896 when it switched to the manufacture of semi-vitreous porcelain. Extant pieces in the East Liverpool Museum of Ceramics include napkin plates, dinnerware, toilet ware, and commemorative pieces. This firm was one of six individual potteries which merged to form the East Liverpool Potteries Company in 1901. After only two years the Halls broke from the merger of the faltering conglomeration and began operations as the Hall China Company (Calhoun 1922: 108, 134; Vodrey 1945: 283).

FIGURE 31. East Liverpool Pottery Company: a. ironstone ware, 1894–1896, ware; b. ironstone ware, 1894–1896, ware, variation of Figure 31a; c. semi-vitreous dinnerware, 1896–1901, ware; d. semi-vitreous dinnerware, 1896–1901, ware, reads "CARSEILLES PORCELAIN."

a

b

c

D. of R.
174.

d

FIGURE 32. East Liverpool Pottery Company: a. semi-vitreous napkin plate, 1896–1901, ware; b. semi-vitreous dinnerware, 1896–1901, ware, same as Figure 32a but without "E.L.P. CO."; c. semi-vitreous dinnerware, 1896–1901, ware; d. semi-vitreous ware, ca. 1898, Barber, (1904: 114), special order for the Daughters of Rebecca.

EAST LIVERPOOL POTTERIES COMPANY (Figures 33–34)   1901–1907 (1933)

In 1901 a merger of six autonomous potteries created the East Liverpool Potteries Company. East Liverpool's Globe Pottery Company, the East Liverpool Pottery Company, Wallace and Chetwynd, the East End Pottery Company, and the George C. Murphy Pottery Company joined with the United States Pottery Company of nearby Wellsville in an effort to compete with the giants of the industry. Silas M. Ferguson, who had been instrumental in the founding of the United States Pottery Company seems to have been the leading force in the merger and became general manager of the new conglomerate (McCord 1905: 172; Geneological and Family History of Eastern Ohio 1903: 468). Although all of the individual firms attempted to use a uniform pottery mark on the semi-vitreous wares they produced, variations do occur in a supposedly "uniform" mark. These subtle differences probably indicate the various component manufacturers of the merger.

In 1903 all of the companies, except the Globe Pottery and the United States Pottery, abandoned the merger and returned to independent operations. In 1907 the East Liverpool Potteries Company ceased to exist as a combination when the Globe and United States potteries announced the end of the merger (The Evening Review 16 January 1907: 1).

However, the end of the merger did not mean the end of the name "East Liverpool Potteries Company." The United States Pottery continued to operate in Wellsville under the above name. This firm produced semi-vitreous table ware, hotel ware, and toilet ware. Even though the name "Potteries" was now a misnomer, the firm used a new pottery mark (see marks section) and named a line of dinnerware "Elpco." In 1936 the firm became the Purinton Pottery Company (Mss. ELMC, Company price list 1921; Crockery and Glass Journal 1917; China and Glass Trade Directory 1927: 16; USPA 1933: 7).

a   b

FIGURE 33. East Liverpool Potteries Company: a. semi-vitreous ware, 1901–ca. 1907, ware, also found with "ANTIQUE" above shield; b. semi-vitreous ware, 1901–ca. 1907, ware, variation of Figure 33a.

a

b

c

FIGURE 34. East Liverpool Potteries Company: a. semi-vitreous dinnerware, ca. 1907–ca. 1925, ware; b. semi-vitre-ous dinnerware, ca. 1907–ca. 1925, ware, variation of Figure 34a; c. semi-vitreous dinnerware, ca. 1925–1933 (1927), ware, see similar mark "CARTWRIGHT BROTHERS" Figure 22c.

MORLEY, GODWIN AND FLENTKE   1855–1878
GODWIN AND FLENTKE (Figure 35a)   1878–1882
WILLIAM FLENTKE (Figure 35b)   1882–1886

Five experienced potters, William Flentke, George and Samuel Morley, James Godwin, and David Colclough, leased the pottery formerly operated by Richard Henderson in 1855. Two years later the partners purchased the plant and named it the "Salamander Pottery Works." By 1861 Colclough and Samuel Morley had withdrawn from the firm, which continued to produce yellow ware and Rockingham. In 1874, Morley, Godwin and Flentke built a large two-story brick building across the street from their original plant and transferred their operation and the "Salamander" name to the new location. The firm manufactured ironstone china exclusively and sold its former pottery to a new company called Flentke (not William), Worcester and Company which renamed the plant "Buckeye." This firm continued to produce Rockingham and yellow ware. Morley, Godwin and Flentke produced plain ironstone and decorated table, hotel, and toilet wares as well as tea sets. They were especially proud of their "Rustic" shape which was manufactured in all of the aforementioned lines (Pioneer 1876; Mss. ELMC, Company price list ca. 1876).

George Morley withdrew from the partnership in 1878 to establish his own pottery in Wellsville. Godwin and Flentke continued to manufacture ironstone until 1882 when Godwin sold his half interest to Flentke. Flentke operated the "Salamander" pottery, producing "Iron Stone China and Fine Decorated Ware," until 1886 when the Standard Pottery Company was organized (Calhoun 1922: 107; Mss. ELMC, Articles of Agreement 17 January 1882, Company price list ca. 1884, Company stationery 5 September 1883; Vodrey 1945: 283).

a

b

FIGURE 35. Godwin and Flentke/William Flentke: a. ironstone dinnerware, 1878–1880, ware; b. ironstone dinnerware, 1882–1886, ware, variation of this mark reads "GODWIN AND FLENTKE," ironstone tableware, 1880–1882, ware.

FRENCH CHINA COMPANY (Figures 36–39)   1898–1929

The French China Company, organized by the Sebring brothers, opened a new pottery in East Liverpool in 1898. It was called "Klondyke" because of its great distance from the center of town. The firm produced semi-porcelain dinner, tea, and toilet wares, as well as "Special novelties." The Sebrings moved the French China Company to a new plant in Sebring, Ohio, in 1901 stating that they left East Liverpool in order to expand and because they were ". . . not content to follow the antiquated methods of a past generation. . . ." At its new location the firm continued to manufacture a quality semi-porcelain product. In 1916 O. H. Sebring created the Sebring Manufacturing Corporation to function as a holding company for French China, the Strong Manufacturing Company, and the Saxon China Company. However, each firm continued to operate independently until 1929 when the holding company joined the American Chinaware Corporation (Illustrated Glass and Pottery World October 1897, April 1898, May 1898; Mss. ELMC, Company catalog 1912; McKee 1966: 41; Mss. ELMC, American Chinaware Corporation, Records of Formation 1929).

a

b

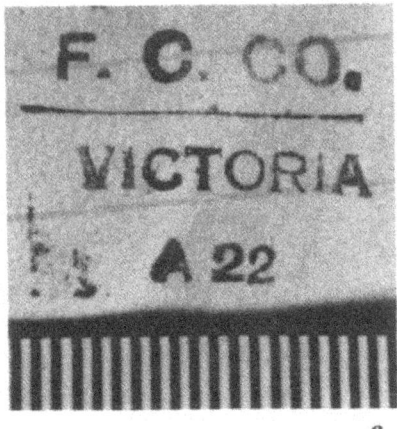

c

FIGURE 36. French China Company: a. semi-vitreous ware, ca. 1916–1929, Modern Stamp; b. semi-vitreous ware, ca. 1916–1929, Modern Stamp; c. semi-vitreous ware, ca. 1916–1929, Modern Stamp.

FIGURE 37. French China Company: a. semi-vitreous dinnerware, ca. 1916–1929, ware; b. semi-vitreous ware, ca. 1916–1929, Modern Stamp; c. semi-vitreous ware, ca. 1916–1929, Modern Stamp.

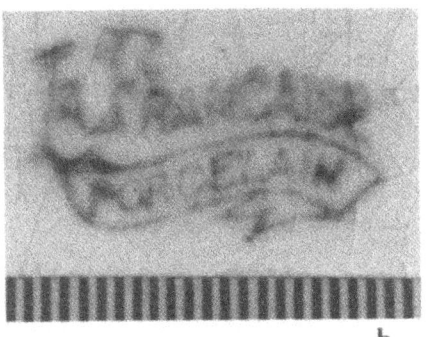

FIGURE 38. French China Company: a. semi-vitreous ware, 1898–ca. 1916, ware; b. semi-vitreous ware, 1898–ca. 1916, ware; c. semi-vitreous toilet ware, 1898–ca. 1916, Barber (1904: 42); d. semi-vitreous toilet ware, 1898–ca. 1916, Barber (1904: 42).

FIGURE 39. French China Company: a. semi-vitreous toilet ware, 1898–ca. 1916, Barber (1904: 42); b. semi-vitreous toilet ware, 1898–ca. 1916, Barber (1904: 42); c. semi-vitreous toilet ware, 1898–ca. 1916, Barber (1904: 42); d. semi-vitreous toilet ware, 1898–ca. 1916, Barber (1904: 42).

GLOBE POTTERY COMPANY (Figures 40–42)   1881–1901/1907–1912

The Globe Pottery Company began as Frederick, Shenkle, Allen and Company in 1881. These local potters constructed a three-story brick pottery consisting of a main building (36' × 100'), three kilns, and assorted ancillary structures. By early 1882 they began operations producing Rockingham and yellow wares. In 1888 Jacob Shenkle and A. B. Allen, in partnership with George and Noah Frederick, reorganized the enterprise as the Globe Pottery Company. The firm added semi-porcelain to its line at this time and by the mid-1890s was also producing Rockingham, cream colored ware, decorated jet ware and teapots, and specialty items (Columbiana County Directory 1881; Crockery, Glass and Lamps 28 February 1896).

The Globe Company joined the short-lived East Liverpool Potteries Company in 1901; upon the demise of the latter in 1907, it returned to independent operation with new corporate officers. During the next few years the company offered a line of semi-porcelain dinner and toilet ware as well as specialty items such as vases, tankards, plaques, trays, and jugs. The Globe Pottery Company gradually declined and finally ceased operations in 1912 after suffering extensive damage during the flood of that year (Glass and Pottery World 1907: 27; The Evening Review 16 January 1907: 1; Calhoun 1922: 131).

FIGURE 40. Globe Pottery Company: a. yellow ware statue (Jumbo/the elephant), 1888–1901, ware, same mark as Figure 40b; b. yellow ware vase, 1888–1901, ware; c. ironstone toilet ware, ca. 1896, ware; d. semi-vitreous specialty ware, ca. 1898, ware.

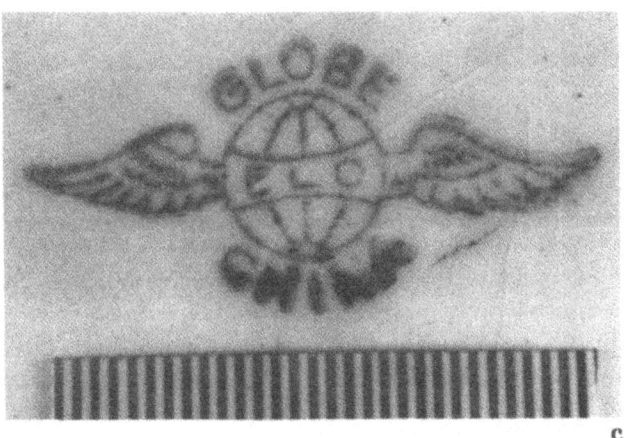

FIGURE 41. Globe Pottery Company: a. semi-vitreous dinnerware, 1888–1901/1907–1912, ware; b. semi-vitreous dinnerware, 1888–1901/1907–1912, ware; c. semi-vitreous dinnerware, 1888–1901/1907–1912, ware.

FIGURE 42. Globe Pottery Company: a. semi-vitreous dinnerware, ca. 1900, Barber (1904: 113); b. semi-vitreous toilet ware, ca. 1898, Barber (1904: 113); c. semi-vitreous hotel ware, ca. 1896, Barber (1904: 113).

GOODWIN POTTERY COMPANY (Figures 43–45)   1844–1853/1863–1865/1872–1913

John Goodwin arrived in East Liverpool from Burslem, England, in 1842. Goodwin, a skilled potter, had no difficulty in securing employment, first working at the recently-established Bennett pottery and later for Benjamin Harker. The following year, Goodwin rented a small three-story frame building from James Blakeley and converted it into a pottery which he dubbed the "Eagle Pottery." About 1845 he added the production of furniture and door knobs to his Rockingham and yellow ware business. Although this aspect of his operation was successful, Goodwin discontinued the production of knobs in 1849 because of stiff competition (Pioneer 1876).

In 1846 Goodwin purchased the Blakeley property for $300.00 and during the next five years completed extensive additions and improvements. He employed about 20 operatives, producing from eight to ten thousand dollars worth of ware annually. In the yellow ware line the firm offered bowls, milk pans, pitchers, chambers, mugs, nappies, and pie plates. Goodwin also manufactured Rockingham ewers, washbowls, spittoons, tea and coffee pots, pitchers, and sugars. He also experimented with creamware. Goodwin sold his "Eagle Pottery" in 1853 to Samuel and William Baggott, retiring temporarily from the pottery business and turning to real estate speculation (Mss. ELMC, Company price list 1850; American Patriot 13 June 1848; Pioneer 1876).

Following a 10 year hiatus, Goodwin built the "Novelty Pottery Works" in 1863 and drew its first kiln of ware in the fall of 1864. He operated this pottery for two years before selling it to the firms of A. J. Marks and Company. John Goodwin again left the pottery business. In 1870, however, he returned to manufacturing in Trenton, New Jersey, when he purchased an interest in the Trenton Pottery Company, manufacturers of ironstone, c.c. ware, and sanitary earthenwares (Pioneer 1876; Barber 1893, reprint ed. 1976: 200).

Goodwin returned to East Liverpool in 1872 and in partnership with his three sons he purchased the "Broadway Pottery Works" from T. Rigby and Company. The partnership established the firm of John Goodwin and Sons. During the next three years, The Goodwins produced Rockingham and yellow ware while overhauling and extending their plant. When John Goodwin died in January 1875, the plant closed for seven months. Goodwin's sons Henry, James, and George reorganized the company as the Goodwin Brothers Pottery Company at its Broadway location. The new firm continued to produce Rockingham and yellow ware (Mss. ELMC, Company price list 1875; Pioneer 1876).

Following extensive remodeling and additions to the plant, the Goodwin brothers began the production of c.c. ware and halted the manufacture of yellow earthenwares. At some point between 1885 and 1891 the company introduced a new line of whiteware which they termed "Pearl White." This exclusive line included hotel ware, dinnerware, cake plates and other accessory pieces, tea sets, and toilet sets (ELT 6 October 1877, 14 June 1884; Mss. ELMC, Company price list 1891).

In 1893 the Goodwin brothers incorporated their firm as the Goodwin Pottery Company. Soon after this they halted the production of c.c. and "Pearl White" wares in favor of ironstone and semi-porcelain. The Goodwin family withdrew its interests from the pottery business in 1913 when they leased their works to the Davidson-Stevenson Porcelain Company (Calhoun 1922: 47, 150; U S P A 1913: 19).

A section of the "Eagle" pottery of Goodwin/Baggott still stands in East Liverpool and was placed on the National Register of Historic Places in 1971. The site presently consists of a single "bottle" kiln (periodic-updraft) and one building.

FIGURE 43. Goodwin Brothers Pottery Company: a. ironstone toilet ware (Pearl White), 1885–ca. 1897, ware; b. ironstone dinnerware (Pearl White), 1885–ca. 1897, ware; c. ironstone dinnerware, 1885–1898, ware; d. ironstone sanitary ware, ca. 1888–1893, ware.

a

b

c

d

FIGURE 44. Goodwin Pottery Company: a. ironstone ware, ca. 1888–1893, Barber (1904: 106); b. ironstone ware, 1893–ca. 1906, ware; c. semi-vitreous dinnerware, 1893–ca. 1906, ware; d. ironstone or semi-vitreous hotel ware, 1893–ca. 1906, Modern Stamp.

FIGURE 45. Goodwin Pottery Company: a. semi-vitreous dinnerware, 1893–ca. 1906, ware; b. semi-vitreous dinnerware, ca. 1906–1913, ware; c. semi-vitreous tableware, ca. 1906–1913, ware, decal.

HALL CHINA COMPANY (Figures 46–63)   1903–PRESENT

In July 1903, the members of the East Liverpool Potteries Company met to distribute the assets of the expiring firm. Robert Hall, Sr. accepted the former West, Hardwick and Company pottery building as his portion of the assets and on 14 August 1903, the Hall China Company was born. The small pottery struggled at first, facing stiff competition from its rivals in the "Crockery City." The company's first products included bed pans, spittoons, combinets, and some dinnerware. Because of the untimely death of his father, Robert T. Hall assumed management of the firm less than two months after its founding (Duke 1977: 8, 12; Company history; ACS, 1945: 280; Evening News Review 26 September 1903: 1).

The Hall China Company developed the first successful leadless glaze in 1911; this allowed them to perfect their single-fire method. This notable achievement, combined with the outbreak of World War I, which prohibited European potteries from producing or shipping the vessels used in food preparation and serving, opened up extensive markets for the company's products. Hall developed its institutional line selling its vitrified fire-proof cooking china to world-wide markets. At various times during the next 30 years, they added kitchen ware, refrigerator ware, specialty items, dinnerware (for a brief period), and teapots to their line. The rapid growth of the company following the perfection of their "secret process" made it necessary to expand. By 1927 the firm had acquired two additional plants, and in 1930 it consolidated all three potteries into a new building located in East Liverpool's East End section. The Hall China Company continues to operate in this building (Company history; Duke 1977: 8, 9; ACS 1945: 280, 281).

A thorough and comprehensive study of Hall China Company products (shapes, styles, colors, dates, etc.) by Harvey Duke is currently available. This publication (see bibliography), while geared toward collectors, can provide archaeologists with excellent information.

a

FIGURE 46. Hall China Company: a. semi-vitreous dinnerware, 1903–1911, ware.

b

c

d

FIGURE 46 continued. b. semi-vitreous dinnerware, 1903–1911, ware; c. semi-vitreous dinnerware, 1903–1911, ware; d. semi-vitreous dinnerware, 1903–1911, ware.

FIGURE 47. Hall China Company: a. vitrified china, 1911–present, ware; b. vitrified china, ca. 1930–present, ware; c. vitrified china, ca. 1930–present, ware; d. vitrified china, ca. 1916–ca. 1930, ware, also found without "MADE IN U.S.A." in circle.

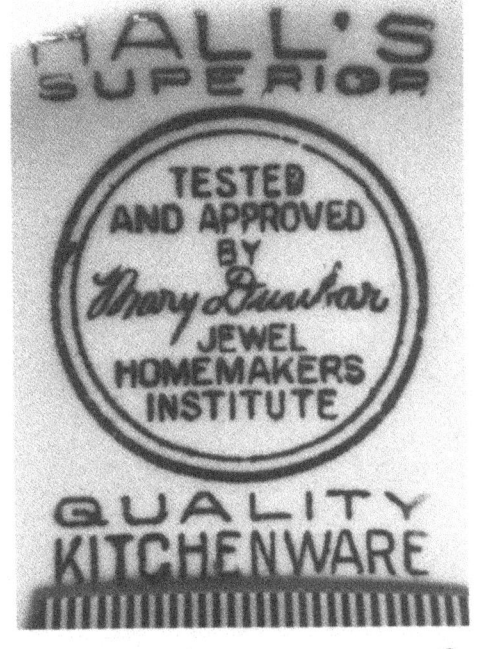

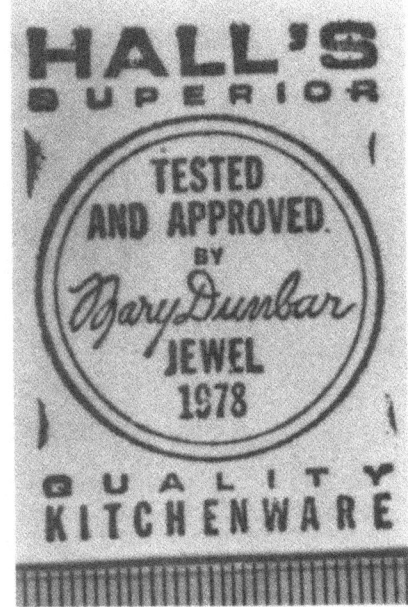

a

b

c

d

FIGURE 48. Hall China Company: a. vitrified kitchen ware, 1932–1978, ware; b. vitrified kitchen ware, 1978–present, company stamp; c. vitrified dinnerware, 1936–1978, "Cameo Rose" ca. 1940–ca. 1965; d. vitrified dinnerware, 1978–present, company stamp.

FIGURE 49. Hall China Company: a. vitrified dinnerware, 1936–ca. 1976, company stamp, also appears without pattern name; b. vitrified dinnerware, 1936–ca. 1953, company stamp, also "GOLDEN OAK PATTERN" AND "SPRINGTIME PATTERN"; c. vitrified kitchenware, 1932–ca. 1963, ware; d. vitrified kitchenware, ca. 1935, ware, impressed, mixing bowls in four different sizes and colors, mostly for the Jewel Tea Company.

Made Exclusively for
WESTINGHOUSE By
The Hall China Co.
MADE IN U.S.A.

a

MADE EXCLUSIVELY FOR
WESTINGHOUSE
BY
The Hall China Co.
MADE IN U. S. A.

b

Made Exclusively for
WESTINGHOUSE By
The Hall China Co.

c

d

FIGURE 50. Hall China Company: a. vitrified refrigerator ware, 1938–ca. 1952, ware; b. vitrified refrigerator ware, 1938–ca. 1952, ware; c. vitrified refrigerator ware, 1938–ca. 1952, ware; d. vitrified refrigerator ware, 1938–ca. 1952, ware.

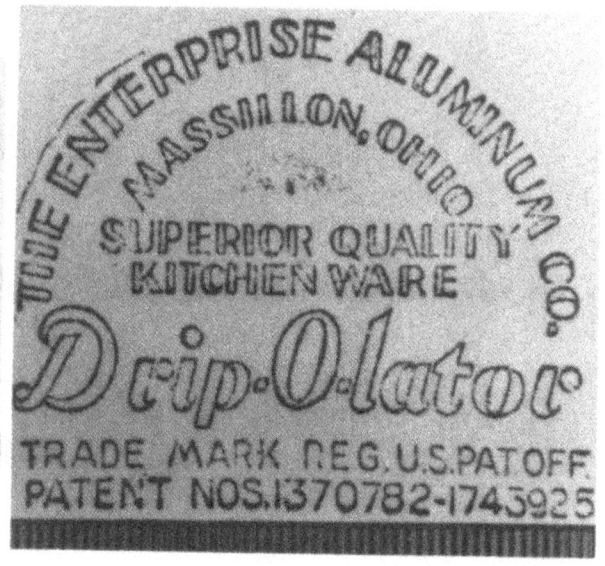

FIGURE 51. Hall China Company: a. vitrified refrigerator ware, ca. 1938, ware; b. vitrified refrigerator ware, 1938–ca. 1941, ware, mark reads "Montgomery Ward & Co."; c. vitrified refrigerator ware, ca. 1937, ware; d. vitrified coffee pots, 1935–ca. 1955, company stamp.

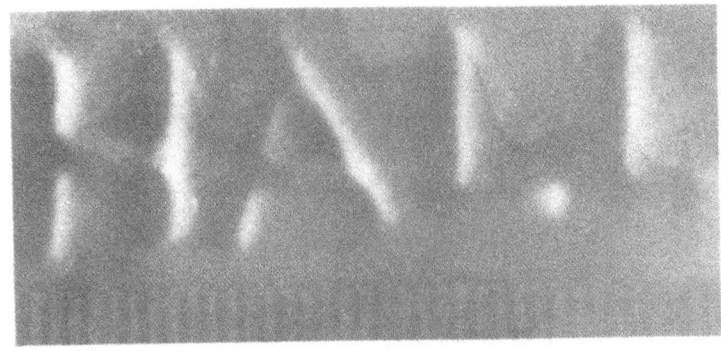

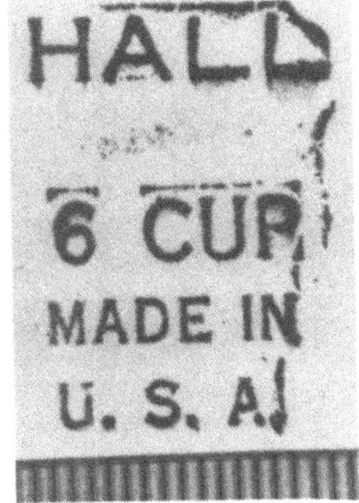

FIGURE 52. Hall China Company: a. vitrified china, 1912–present, ware, impressed; b. vitrified china, 1936–ca. 1958, company stamp, pictured mark 1956, other marks do not have "100 ANNIVERSARY"; c. vitrified teapots, 1918–ca. 1976, company stamp, a number would appear in the space between "HALL" and "6 cup"; d. vitrified china premium, ca. 1940, company stamp.

FIGURE 53. Hall China Company: a. vitrified china, ca. 1931–1978, ware; b. vitrified china, ca. 1931–1978, ware.

c

d

FIGURE 53 continued. c. vitrified teapot, ca. 1940–ca. 1957, Quality Stamp; d. vitrified teapot, ca. 1957–present, company stamp.

FIGURE 54. Hall China Company: a. vitrified kitchen ware, 1978–1979, Quality Stamp; b. vitrified cheese crock, ca. 1952–ca. 1957, Quality Stamp; c. vitrified cheese crock, ca. 1957–present, Quality Stamp; d. vitrified china, 1920–1960, company stamp.

FIGURE 55. Hall China Company: a. vitrified hotel ware, ca. 1945, company stamp; b. vitrified hotel ware, 1981, company stamp.

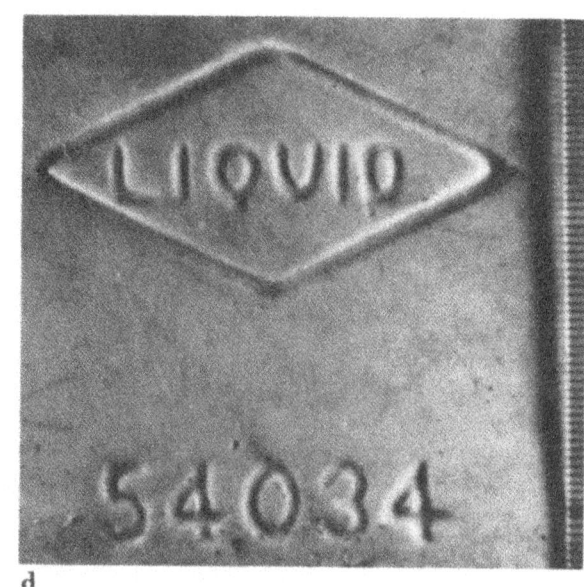

FIGURE 55 continued. c. vitrified soda fountain ware, 1926–ca. 1954, ware, impressed; d. vitrified soda fountain ware, ca. 1954, ware, impressed.

a

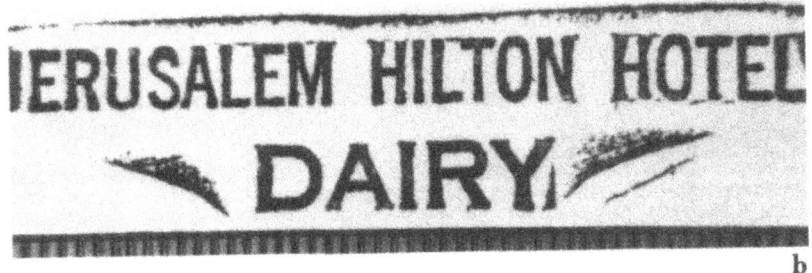

b

c

d

FIGURE 56. Hall China Company: a. vitrified hotel ware, ca. 1932–present, company stamp, Kosher food mark; b. vitrified hotel ware, ca. 1932–present, company stamp, Kosher food mark; c. vitrified dinnerware, 1938–ca. 1953, ware, "HARMONY HOUSE" Brand name for Sears; patterns also "Richmond" and "Monticello"; d. vitrified hotel ware, ca. 1945, company stamp, "G.M.T. CO." is a hotel supply company.

FIGURE 57. Hall China Company: a. vitrified teapot, 1907–present, ware; b. vitrified dinnerware, ca. 1945, company stamp; c. vitrified cooking ware, ca. 1950–present, company stamp; d. vitrified hotel ware, ca. 1955, company stamp.

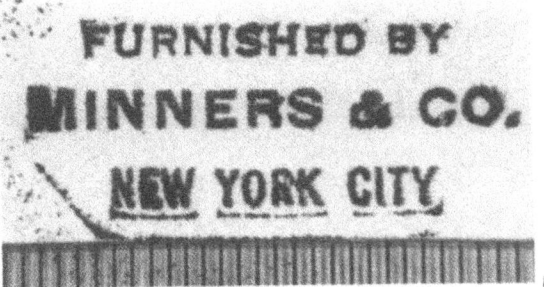

FIGURE 58. Hall China Company: a. vitrified hotel ware, ca. 1955–ca. 1965, company stamp, "MINNERS & CO." hotel supply company; b. vitrified china premium, ca. 1955, company stamp, drug store suppliers; c. vitrified hotel ware, ca. 1955, company stamp; d. vitrified hotel ware, ca. 1955, company stamp.

FIGURE 59. Hall China Company: a. vitrified household cooking ware, ca. 1950–ca. 1955, company stamp; b. vitrified ware, 1952–1968, company stamp, used on "Hallcraft," by Eva Zeisel; c. vitrified hotel cooking and serving ware, ca. 1957, company stamp; d. vitrified dinnerware, ca. 1957–ca. 1973, Quality Stamp.

FIGURE 60. Hall China Company: a. vitrified dinnerware, 1952–ca. 1968, company stamp; b. ironstone-type, ca. 1957–1977, company stamp, "REDCLIFF" was a distributor.

c

d

FIGURE 60 continued. c. vitrified cooking ware, ca. 1965, Quality Stamp; d. vitrified hotel ware, ca. 1960–present, Quality Stamp.

FIGURE 61. Hall China Company: a. vitrified serving ware, ca. 1957–circa 1965, Quality Stamp; b. vitrified hotel ware, ca. 1970, company stamp.

c

HALL CHINA
OVEN-PROOF GOLDEN GLO

Start with cold oven. Heat gradually to desired temperature. Wash by hand with mild soap. Do not use abrasives or detergents.

d

FIGURE 61 continued. c. vitrified ware, ca. 1970, company stamp, any "Hall" ware decorated completely in gold is "GOLDEN GLO"; d. vitrified ware, ca. 1970, company stamp, any "Hall" ware decorated completely in gold is "GOLDEN GLO."

a

b

c

FIGURE 62. Hall China Company: a. vitrified hotel ware, ca. 1978, company stamp; b. vitrified ware, 1973–present, company stamp, series item; c. vitrified hotel ware, ca. 1975, company stamp.

FIGURE 63. Hall China Company: a. vitrified china, 1972–present, Quality Stamp; b. ironstone, circa 1970, Quality Stamp, British imported ware; c. vitrified china, 1972–present, ware.

HARKER ASSOCIATIONS (Figures 64–77)

Benjamin Harker, Sr. emigrated from England in 1839 and upon his arrival in East Liverpool he purchased 50 acres of land from Abel Coffin near the fledgling town. Harker's purchase turned out to be a very fortuitous investment as the land was rich in clay deposits. He sold clay to interested parties in Pittsburgh and reputedly supplied James Bennett with clay for the town's first pottery. Although he was not a potter, Harker opened East Liverpool's second pottery in 1840 and leased it to Edward Tunnicliff and John Whetton. This arrangement was not successful and in 1842 Tunnicliff was joined by John Goodwin and Thomas Croxall. These skilled potters produced earthenware for a short time, but this firm was soon dissolved by mutual consent. Harker then decided to try it on his own and hired Goodwin to train his sons, Benjamin, Jr. and George S. in the pottery trade (Mss. ELMC, Deed 22 August 1839; Pioneer 1876).

The Harkers operated this small pottery until about 1846 when James Taylor entered the firm. The new partnership, Harker, Taylor and Company, constructed a large three-story brick pottery which they named "Etruria" after Wedgewood's famous English works. In 1848 they were manufacturing a variety of ware, including door knobs, toys, and ceramic tile for hearths and table tops. Harker, Taylor and Company also produced Rockingham of an exceptional quality, hound-handled pitchers being the most notable. In 1850 the firm won a silver medal for its Rockingham from the Massachusetts Charitable Mechanic Association. Taylor and Henry Speeler, who also worked at the pottery, left East Liverpool for Trenton, New Jersey in 1851 to establish their own pottery (Pioneer 1876; American Patriot 20 June 1848; Silver Medal 1850).

In 1851 Ezekiel Creighton and Mathew Thompson joined George S. Harker in his enterprise. Thompson, a wealthy merchant, provided much-needed capital and business expertise. This new company produced a high-quality yellow ware and Rockingham; however, the new partnership was ephemeral. The local newspaper reported in 1854 that ". . . Harker, Thompson and Co. was dissolved on the 11th day of April last, by the death of Ezekiel Creighton." Harker and Thompson continued the operation of the firm under the name George S. Harker and Company (WP 22 July 1851, 30 May 1854; United States Census 1850).

Benjamin Harker Jr. left the Harker, Thompson partnership in 1853 and with William Smith established a pottery firm in the former "Mansion House Pottery" of Salt and Mear. Harker and Smith employed about 30 workers and produced Rockingham and yellow wares. Depressed business conditions during the mid-1850s forced the dissolution of the partnership in 1855 and Benjamin Harker, Jr. regained his former interest in the original "Etruria" pottery. In 1877 he and his sons established the "Wedgewood Pottery" and began the production of c.c. ware. Evidently, Harker's sons were not too interested in the manufacture of pottery and in 1881 the plant was sold to the firm of Wallace and Chetwynd (WP 29 November 1853, 13 February 1855; Calhoun 1922: 122).

Meanwhile George S. Harker continued to manufacture Rockingham and yellow ware at the "Etruria" pottery. In July 1864 George S. died, and David Boyce, his bother-in-law, was employed to manage the firm until George's sons were old enough to operate the plant. This marks the beginning of a long relationship because the Boyce family remained associated with the Harker Pottery Company until it closed. By 1876 the firm operated four kilns making it one of the largest potteries in East Liverpool at the time (Pioneer 1876).

When Benjamin Jr. left the firm in 1877 to establish the "Wedgewood" pottery, W. W. Harker, George's son, took over management of the company. The firm name of George S. Harker and Company was retained. In 1879 the firm discontinued the production of Rockingham and yellow ware and began manufacturing white ironstone and by 1880 was offering two toilet ware shapes, tea sets, dinner ware, and accessory pieces such as tureens, bakers, and casseroles. Incorporated in 1890 as the Harker Pottery Company, it soon after began to produce semi-porcelain goods rather than ironstone. In 1911 the company acquired the former plant of the National China Company and operated both plants until 1931 when it purchased the abandoned pottery of Edwin M. Knowles in Chester, West Virginia. At this time the corporation was producing vitreous dinnerware, hotel ware, toilet sets, and advertising novelties (Columbiana County Directory 1881: 862; Mss. ELMC, Company price list 1880; Vodrey 1945: 285; China and Glass Trade Directory 1927).

From 1930 to 1970 the Harker Pottery Company produced a wide range of domestic dinnerware, ovenware, and cooking ware patterns. Some of the better known styles were "Cameo ware," "White Rose," "Bakerite," and "HotOven." In 1972 the Harker Pottery Company ceased operations (Grace Mahon 1981, pers. comm.).

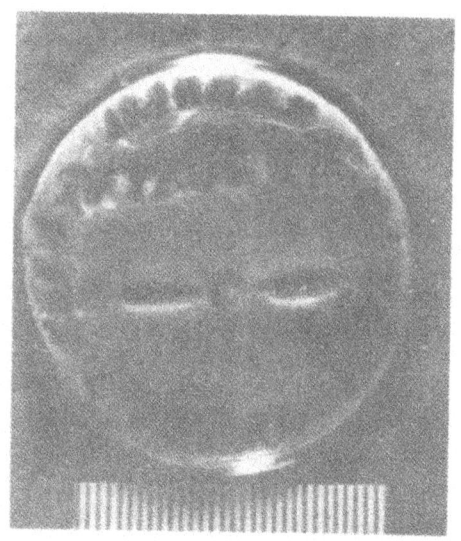

a

b

FIGURE 64. Harker Pottery Company: a. Rockingham hound-handled pitcher, 1846–1851, ware, impressed on raised medallion "Harker Taylor Co. East Liverpool, Ohio;" b. This figure represents Figure 64a illustrating the impressed mark, Barber (1904: 105).

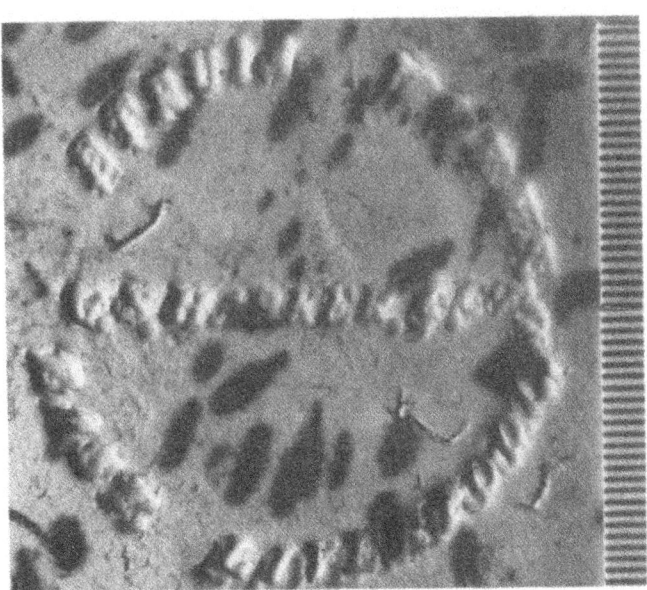

FIGURE 64 continued. c. Rockingham cuspidor, ca. 1862, ware, impressed, mark reads: "ETRURIA WORKS/1862/ EAST LIVERPOOL"; d. Rockingham cuspidor, 1860–1879, ware impressed, mark reads: "ETRURIA WORKS/G S HARKER & CO./EAST LIVERPOOL O."

b

c

d

FIGURE 65. Harker Pottery Company: a. ironstone tableware, 1879–1890, ware; b. ironstone ware, 1879–1890, ware; c. ironstone ware, 1879–1890, ware, size variation of Figure 65b; d. ironstone ware, 1879–1890, ware.

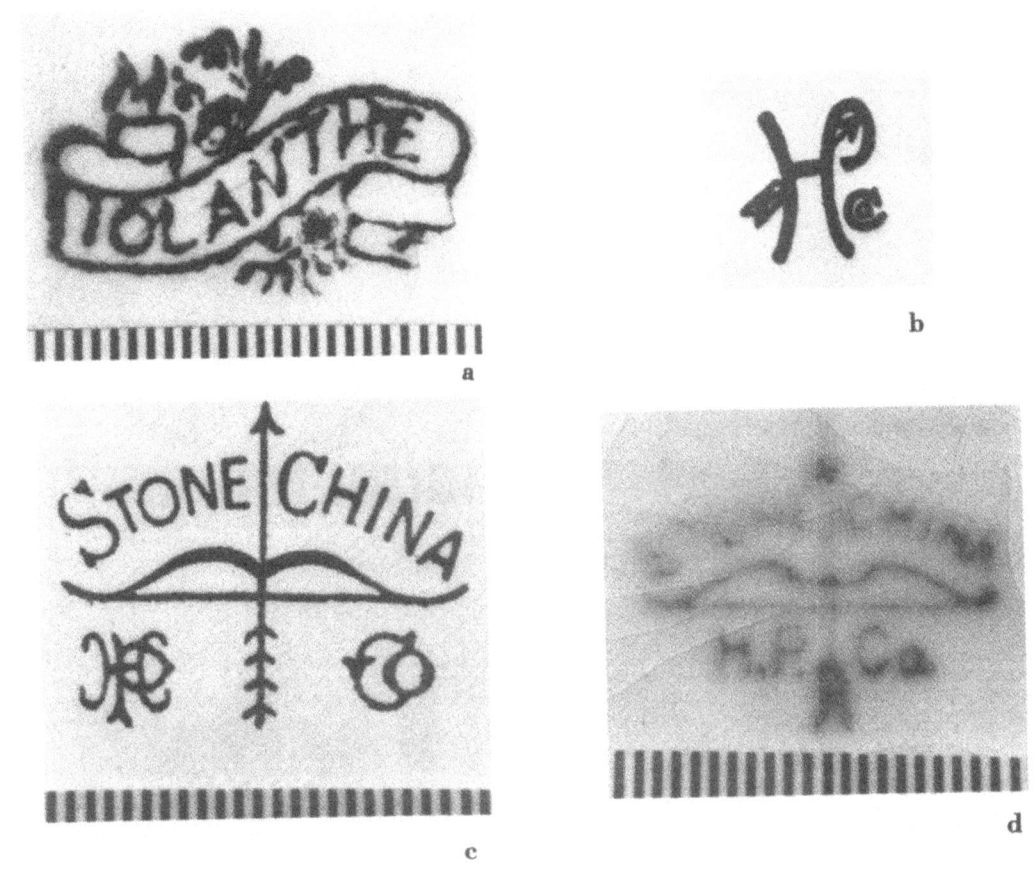

FIGURE 66. Harker Pottery Company: a. ironstone toilet ware, 1879–1890, ware; b. ironstone or semi-vitreous ware, 1890–1904, Barber (1904: 105); c. ironstone ware, 1890–ca. 1900, ware; d. ironstone ware, 1890–ca. 1910, ware.

FIGURE 67. Harker Pottery Company: a. ironstone or vitreous hotel ware, 1890–ca. 1920, ware; b. semi-vitreous ware, 1890–1930, ware; c. semi-vitreous ware, 1930–ca. 1945, ware.

FIGURE 68. Harker Pottery Company: a. semi-vitreous dinnerware, 1910–1935, ware; b. semi-vitreous dinnerware, ca. 1930–1935, ware, mark in color; c. semi-vitreous oven ware, ca. 1935–ca. 1950, ware; d. semi-vitreous kitchen and oven ware, ca. 1935, ware.

FIGURE 69. Harker Pottery Company: a. semi-vitreous refrigerator and cooking ware, 1935–ca. 1950, ware; b. semi-vitreous dinnerware, 1935–ca. 1950, ware, mark in color.

FIGURE 70. Harker Pottery Company: a. semi-vitreous dinnerware, ca. 1930–ca. 1940, ware.

FIGURE 70 continued. b. semi-vitreous dinner and oven ware, 7/1940–ca. 1948, ware; c. semi-vitreous dinner and oven ware, 7/1940–ca. 1948, ware; d. semi-vitreous ware, 1939–1947, ware.

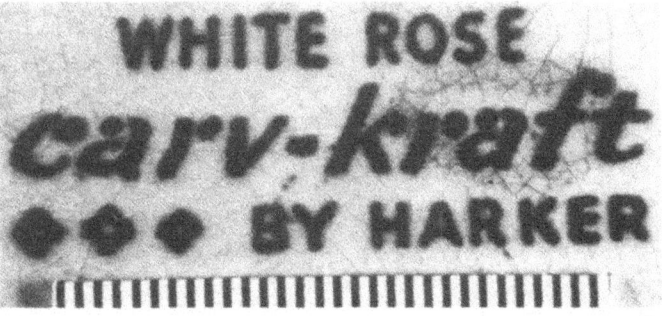

FIGURE 71. Harker Pottery Company: a. semi-vitreous ware, 1948–1963, ware; b. stoneware-type dinnerware, ca. 1950, ware, also "COUNTRY STYLE"; c. stoneware-type dinnerware, ca. 1950–ca. 1960, Quality Stamp; d. semi-vitreous tableware, ca. 1950, ware.

FIGURE 72. Harker Pottery Company: a. semi-vitreous ware, ca. 1955–ca. 1965, ware; b. semi-vitreous ware, 1955–1965, Quality Stamp; c. semi-vitreous ware, ca. 1950, Quality Stamp; d. semi-vitreous ware, ca. 1944, Quality Stamp.

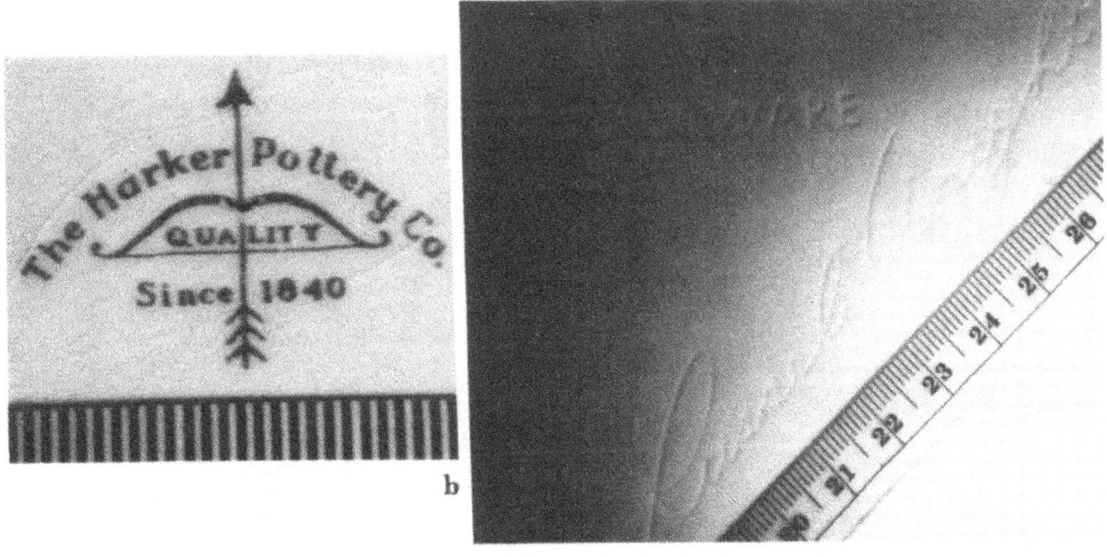

FIGURE 73. Harker Pottery Company: a. semi-vitreous ware, ca. 1950, ware; b. semi-vitreous ware, ca. 1950, ware, decal; c. semi-vitreous ware, ca. 1948–ca. 1955, ware; d. semi-vitreous ware, 1953–1955, ware, impressed mark reads: "HARKERWARE/by/Russel Wright."

FIGURE 74. Harker Pottery Company; a. semi-vitreous ware, 1952–ca. 1960, Quality Stamp; b. semi-vitreous dinner-ware, 1955–ca. 1960, ware; c. semi-vitreous dinnerware, 1955–ca. 1960, ware, size variation Figure 74d; d. semi-vitreous dinnerware, 1955–ca. 1960, ware, variation of Figure 74c.

FIGURE 75. Harker Pottery Company: a. semi-vitreous ware, ca. 1959, ware; b. semi-vitreous dinnerware, ca. 1950–ca. 1960, ware; c. Rockingham (semi-vitreous reproduction), ca. 1965, ware, impressed.

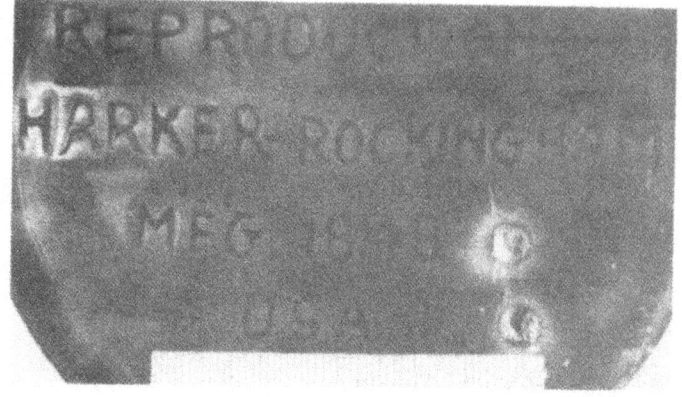

d

FIGURE 75 continued. d. Rockingham (semi-vitreous reproduction), ca. 1965, ware, impressed.

a

b

FIGURE 76. Harker Pottery Company: a. semi-vitreous dinnerware, ca. 1960, ware; b. semi-vitreous ware, 1954–ca. 1965, ware, impressed.

c

d

FIGURE 76 continued. c. stone china, 1954–1972, ware, impressed; d. stone china, 1954–1972, ware, impressed, variation of Figure 76c.

FIGURE 77. Harker Pottery Company: a. semi-vitreous dinnerware, 1960–1972, ware; b. semi-vitreous dinnerware, 1960–1972, ware, mark in color; c. semi-vitreous cooking ware, ca. 1965, Quality Stamp; d. semi-vitreous dinnerware, ca. 1960–1972, ware.

RICHARD HARRISON AND COMPANY (Figure 78)   ca. 1853

Information concerning Richard Harrison is sketchy. Based on the single extant piece of ware at the East Liverpool Museum of Ceramics and sources such as U.S. Census schedules and eyewitness accounts, a time frame in which Harrison was in East Liverpool has been determined.

The first mention of Richard Harrison dates to late 1849 when Richard Henderson established a small two-story pottery in East Liverpool for the production of Rockingham and yellow ware. The firm had barely become operational when Richard Harrison was taken in as a partner. However, after only one year, the pottery was closed. The 1850 census lists Harrison as being an English potter, 36 years of age, with two sons and a daughter. Harrison's eight year-old son, John, was born in England. His two year-old daughter was born in Ohio. Therefore, it can be surmised that the Harrison family arrived in East Liverpool sometime between 1842 and 1848 (United States Census 1850, Columbiana County, Ohio, Liverpool Township: 110; Pioneer 1876).

In the fall of 1852 John Harrison and his sons, Richard and Benjamin, established a pottery in East Liverpool. But this enterprise was also short-lived because the pottery was acquired by Alex Young after only a few years (Pioneer 1876).

FIGURE 78. Richard Harrison and Company: a. Rockingham chamber pot, ca. 1853, ware, impressed on raised medallion.

JOHNSON CHINA COMPANY (Figure 79)   1931–1936

   The Johnson China Company succeeded the unsuccessful American Chinaware Corporation
in the former Smith-Phillips China Company building in 1931. The pottery was located five
miles from the downtown area in the East End or ''Klondyke'' section of East Liverpool. By
1933 the company operated seven kilns and manufactured ''High Grade Chinawares.'' In that
same year, the firm began to face financial difficulties and in January 1937 it filed for bankruptcy
and sold all of its holdings (Mss. ELMC, Appraisal report, Johnson China Company 1933,
Company correspondence 4 February 1936; East Liverpool Review 26 January 1937).

a

b

c

d

FIGURE 79. Johnson China Company: a. semi-vitreous dinnerware, 1931–1936, ware; b. semi-vitreous dinnerware,
1931–1936, ware; c. semi-vitreous dinnerware, 1931–1936, ware; d. semi-vitreous dinnerware, 1931–1936, ware,
possibly not a production mark.

KASS CHINA COMPANY (Figure 80)   1935–1978

Originally an East Liverpool pottery worker, John B. Kass left the potteries in 1923 because of ill health. He then began a shoe business under the name of the John Kass Company and later the Kass Shoe Store. In 1935, he purchased equipment and began a back-yard pottery operation. The Kass China Company manufactured novelties, tea ware, vitrified china, fancy ware, and specialties. The business halted operations totally in 1978 (ELCD 1921: 22, 1926: 904, 1934: 198, 1978: 98, 210; East Liverpool Review 6 September 1940: 11).

a

b

FIGURE 80. Kass China Company: a. semi-vitreous flatware and specialty ware, 1935–1978, ware; b. semi-vitreous specialty ware, 1935–1978, ware.

KEYSTONE CHINA COMPANY (Figure 81)   ca. 1946–1954

This short-lived company began operations sometime around 1946 with Frank Hoskinson as president. They are listed in the city directory as manufacturers and decorators of artware and china. The Keystone China Company produced decorated flatware, novelties and specialties. The company discontinued business in 1954 (East Liverpool Review 20 June 1949; ELCD 1950: 48, 1955: 91).

FIGURE 81. Keystone China Company: a. semi-vitreous dinnerware, 1950–1952, ware; b. semi-vitreous dinnerware, 1952–1954, ware.

EDWIN M. KNOWLES CHINA COMPANY (Figures 82–96)   1900–1963

Edwin Knowles, the youngest son of Isaac W. Knowles (one of the founders of Knowles, Taylor and Knowles) began his own pottery in 1900. In May of that year it was announced that Knowles, along with C. A. Smith and Albert G. Mason, were forming a corporation with capital stock of $100,000 to be known as the "Knowles China Company." The firm erected a new plant in Chester, West Virginia, a town directly across the Ohio River from East Liverpool to manufacture semi-vitreous dinner services, toilet wares, cuspidors, and "Ohio" covered jugs. Although the pottery itself was in Chester, the firm maintained offices in East Liverpool and used that location in its advertisements (Illustrated Glass and Pottery World May 1900: 13; Glass and Pottery World 1909).

In 1913 the company built a 15 kiln plant in Newell, West Virginia, just south of Chester. This pottery was considered the most modern and best designed operation in the district. Both factories were operated until 1931 when the Chester buildings were sold to the Harker Pottery Company, and all operations were moved to the Newell plant. By 1940 the Edwin M. Knowles China Company was the third largest in the United States and employed nine hundred operatives. The firm prospered for many years; however, in September 1962 the management issued the following statement: "Due to the present tariff policies which encourage increasing imports of foreign dinnerware produced with low labor costs, it does not seem possible for the operation of the company to become profitable in the foreseeable future." The firm ceased operations shortly after this (Calhoun 1922: 140; East Liverpool Review 26 March 1940, 4 September 1962, 1 February 1963).

Although a series of "collector" plates are currently being issued under the guise of the Edwin M. Knowles China Company, Chester, West Virginia, these editions are Knowles in name only. The rights to the use of the trade name were purchased by an unrelated corporation. This firm, which is not associated with the East Liverpool ceramic district, is a distributor only.

FIGURE 82. Edwin M. Knowles China Company: a. vitreous ware, 1900–1948, ware; b. semi-vitreous ware, 1900–1948, ware.

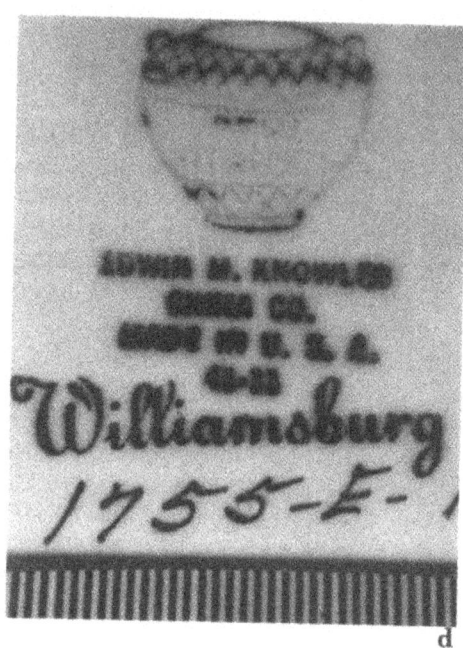

FIGURE 82 continued. c. semi-vitreous ware, 1930–1948, ware; d. semi-vitreous dinnerware, 1941–1948, ware.

FIGURE 83. Edwin M. Knowles China Company: a. semi-vitreous dinnerware, 1910–1948, ware; b. semi-vitreous dinnerware, ca. 1932, ware, also "MAYGLOW," 1930 and "ALICE ANN," 1926.

FIGURE 83 continued. c. semi-vitreous dinnerware, ca. 1938, ware; d. semi-vitreous dinnerware, ca. 1937, ware.

a

b

c

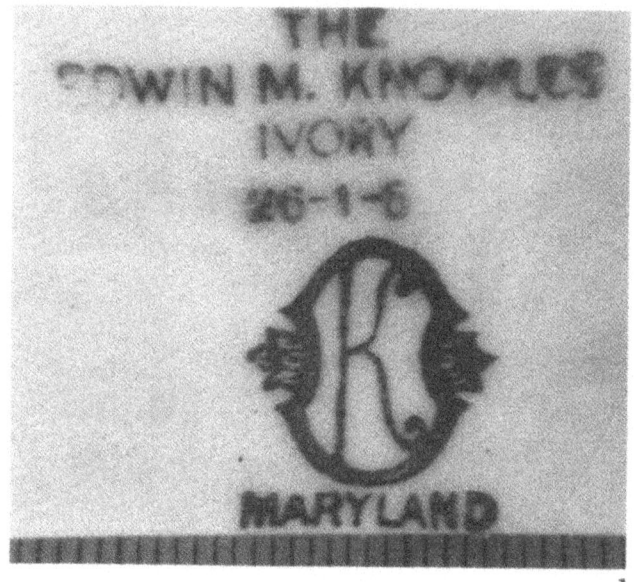

d

FIGURE 84. Edwin M. Knowles China Company: a. semi-vitreous ware, ca. 1905, Barber (1904: 117); b. semi-vitreous dinnerware, ca. 1927, ware; c. semi-vitreous dinnerware, ca. 1925–ca. 1931, ware, also "CAMEO," 1930 and "MARION," 1932; d. semi-vitreous dinnerware, 1923–ca. 1926, ware.

FIGURE 85. Edwin M. Knowles China Company: a. semi-vitreous dinnerware (yellow glaze), 1929, Quality Stamp; b. semi-vitreous dinnerware (pink glaze), 1929, Quality Stamp; c. semi-vitreous dinnerware (green glaze), 1929, Quality Stamp; d. semi-vitreous dinnerware, ca. 1935, ware.

FIGURE 86. Edwin M. Knowles China Company: a. semi-vitreous kitchenware, 1939–ca. 1948, ware; b. semi-vitreous dinnerware, 1934, ware, also "DELANO" and "SYLVAN SATIN"; c. semi-vitreous dinnerware, 1934, ware.

FIGURE 87. Edwin M. Knowles China Company: a. semi-vitreous dinnerware, 1948–1963, ware; b. semi-vitreous dinnerware, 1948–1963, ware; c. semi-vitreous dinnerware, 1951–ca. 1954, ware; d. semi-vitreous dinnerware, ca. 1952, company catalog, also "MOSS ROSE."

FIGURE 88. Edwin M. Knowles China Company: a. semi-vitreous dinnerware, ca. 1953, ware; b. semi-vitreous dinnerware, 1960–1963, company catalog; c. semi-vitreous dinnerware, 1955, company catalog, also "SWEETHEART
ROSE," 1954–1955; d. semi-vitreous dinnerware, 1960–1963, company catalog.

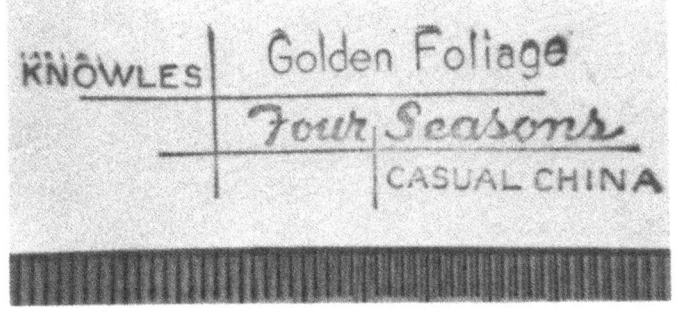

FIGURE 89. Edwin M. Knowles China Company

a. semi-vitreous dinnerware, 1960–1963, company catalog

Pattern	Shape	Year
Golden Foliage	Four Seasons	1960–1963
Leaf Dane	Four Seasons	1960–1963
Reflection	Four Seasons	1960–1963

b. semi-vitreous dinnerware, 1959–1963, company catalog.

Pattern	Shape	Year
Modern Classic	Four Seasons	1960–1963
Ring-A-Round	Four Seasons	1959–1963
Four Seasons White	Four Seasons	1959–1963

c. semi-vitreous dinnerware, ca. 1957–1963, ware, also "MAYFLOWER."

FIGURE 90. Edwin M. Knowles China Company.
a. semi-vitreous dinnerware, ca. 1955, company catalog.

Pattern	Shape	Year
Berkeley	Williamsburg	ca. 1955
Festival	Williamsburg	ca. 1955
Flora	Williamsburg	ca. 1955
Navarra	Williamburg	ca. 1955
Romance	Regent	ca. 1955

b. semi-vitreous dinnerware, 1956, 1957, ware.

Pattern	Shape	Year
Botanica	Esquire	1957
Grass	Russel Wright	1956
Mayfair	Esquire	1957
Queen Anne's Lace	Russel Wright	1956
Seeds	Russel Wright	1956
Snowflower	Russel Wright	1956

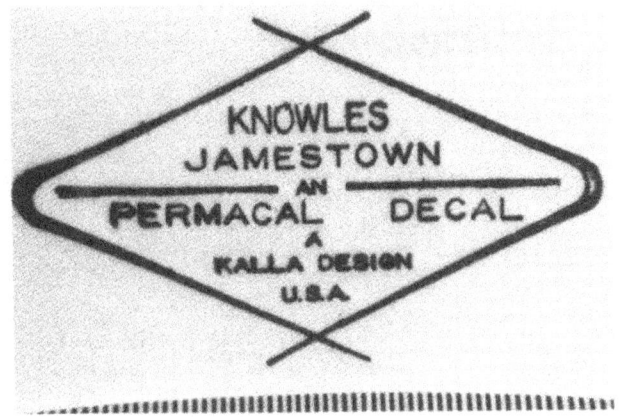

a

b

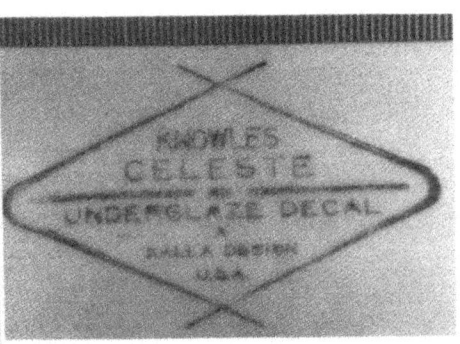

c

FIGURE 91. Edwin M. Knowles China Company.
a–b. semi-vitreous dinnerware, 1961–1963, ware.

Pattern	Shape	Year
a. Jamestown	Tempo	1961–1963
b. Duet	Tempo	1961–1963
Mantilla	Tempo	1961–1963
Provincial Bouquet	Tempo	1961–1963
Tuliptime	Tempo	1961–1963

c. semi-vitreous dinnerware, 1961–1963, ware.

Pattern	Shape	Year
Celeste	Tempo	1961–1963
Debussy	Tempo	1961–1963
Foliage	Tempo	1961–1963
Rodelay	Tempo	1961–1963
Williamsburg	Tempo	1961–1963

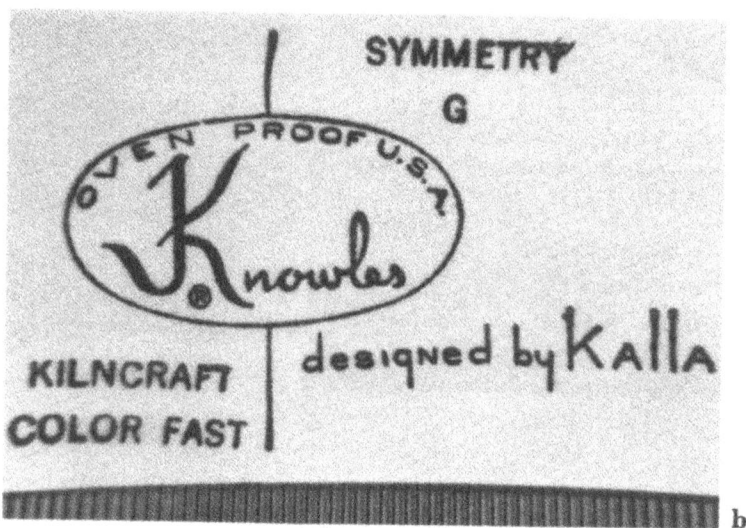

FIGURE 92. Edwin M. Knowles China Company.

a. semi-vitreous dinnerware, 1959, company catalog.

Pattern	Shape	Year
Black-eyed Susan	Forcast	1959
Greenbriar	Forcast	1959
September Song	Forcast	1959
Southwind	Forcast	1959

b. semi-vitreous dinnerware, 1959, company catalog.

Pattern	Shape	Year
Fjord	Americana	1959
Fleurette	Tempo	ca. 1959
Nordic Flower	Americana	1959
Skylark	Americana	1959
Sunburst	Tempo	1959
Symmetry	Tempo	ca. 1959
Victoria	Americana	1959

FIGURE 93. Edwin M. Knowles China Company: semi-vitreous dinnerware, 1948, ware.

Pattern	Shape	Year
Ambassador	Regent	1948
Buttercup		1948
Columbia	Williamsburg	1948
Coronado		1948
Dubarry	Regent	1948
Eldorado		1948
Flora		1948
Florida	Williamsburg	1948
Garland	Williamsburg	1948
Isabella		1948
Lido	Regent	1948
Poppy		1948
Rosemont	Victoria	1948
Severs Blue		1948
Tradition	Regent	1948
Wild Rose	Regent	1948

FIGURE 94. Edwin M. Knowles China Company: semi-vitreous dinnerware, 1955–1957, company catalog.

Pattern	Shape	Year
Chalet	Accent	1955
Equation	Criterion Antique	1955
Fantasy	Accent	1955
Festival	Forcast	1957
Flight	Forcast	1957
Gourmet	Accent	1956
Happy Days	Forcast	1957
Highlands	Criterion	1956
High Serria	Accent	1955
Lacquer Blossom	Accent	1957
Park lane	Heritage	1955
Pretty Pinks	Accent	1957
Star Bright	Accent	1957
Stratosphere	Forcast	1957
Suburbia	Forcast	1956
Weathervane	Forcast	1957
Wild Oats		1955

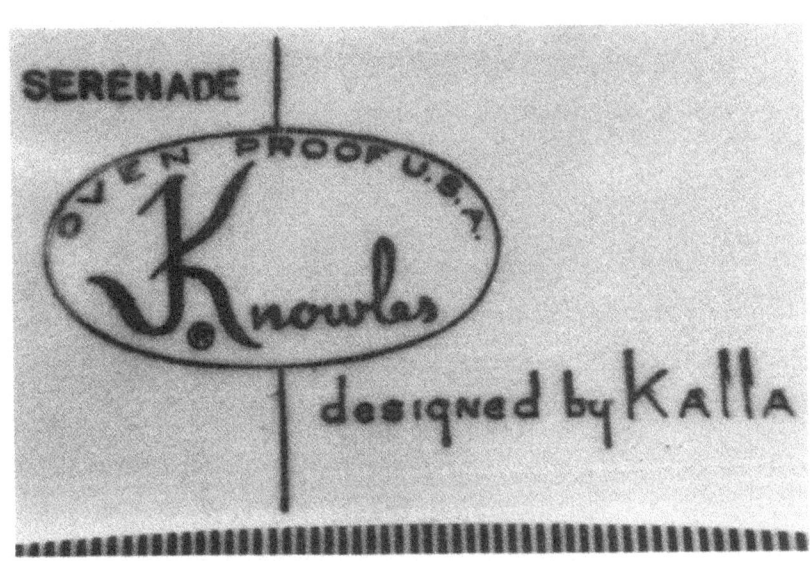

FIGURE 95. Edwin M. Knowles China Company: semi-vitreous dinnerware, 1957, 1958, 1960, ware.

Pattern	Shape	Year
Allure	Classique	1960
Blossomtime	Accent	1958
Breath O' Spring	Classique	1960
Carmen	Accent	1958
Dawn Rose	Americana	1958
Delft	Americana	1957
Evening Song	Classique	1960
Garden Magic	Classique	1960
Golden Wreath	Accent	1960
Lucerne	Classique	1960
Pink Dogwood	Classique	1960
Rhondo	Americana	1958
Royal Brocade	Forcast	1957
Sea Fare	Forcast	1957
Serenade	Classique	1960
Sun Glow	Forcast	1958
Wood Echo	Forcast	1957

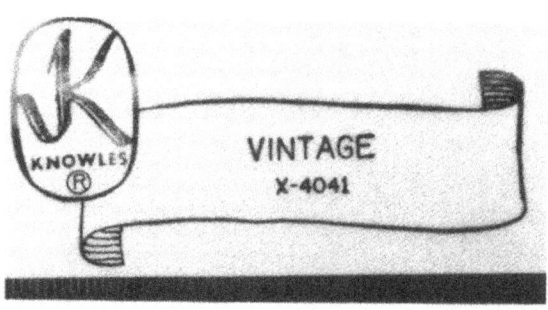

FIGURE 96. Edwin M. Knowles: semi-vitreous dinnerware, 1953–1955, 1957, ware.

Pattern	Shape	Year
Blue Bells	Accent	ca. 1954
Blue Bonnett	Accent	1954
Brown Leaf	Accent	1954
Caprice	Accent	ca. 1954
Carlton	Heritage	1955
Cattails	Accent	1955
Celestial	Criterion	1955
Choreography	Criterion	1955
Classic	Essex	1954–1955
Coral Pine	Criterion	1954
Corsage	Lyric	1954
Country Fair (by Lois Long)	Criterion	1955
Damask Rose	Accent	1954
Dubonnet	Criterion	1955
Ebonite	Criterion	ca. 1954
Ebonite	Tid-bit-tray	1955
Feather Fantasy	Criterion	1955
Fleur de Lis	Criterion	1955
Frosted Leaves	Mayfair	1955
Hen Party, green	Lyric	1954
Hors-d'oeuvres	Accent	1955
Ingrid	Regent	1954
Leaf Ballet (by Freda Diamond)	Accent	1953–1954
Meadow Gold	Criterion	1954
Ming Tree	Accent	ca. 1954
Moss Rose	Criterion	1954
Oakleaf	Criterion	1955
Oslo	Mayfair	1954
Peach Blossom	Accent	1955
Ribbon	Criterion	1954
Rose Tree	Criterion	1955
Scandia	Accent	1954
Scroll	Accent	1955
Silver Spray	Accent	1954
Simplicity	Accent	1955
Sunnybrook Farm	Accent	1957
Tea Rose	Accent	ca. 1954
Tiffany	Accent	1955
Twin Oaks	Accent	ca. 1954
Vintage	Accent	1953–1954
Wheat (by Freda Diamond)	Accent	1954
Wheat Sheaf	Criterion	1955
Wood Violets	Accent	ca. 1954

KNOWLES ASSOCIATIONS   1854–1870
KNOWLES, TAYLOR AND KNOWLES (Figures 97–109)   1870–1929

The firm of Knowles, Taylor and Knowles, (K.T. & K.) was founded in 1854 when Isaac Knowles, a cabinetmaker and carpenter by trade, and Isaac Harvey began operations in a small single-kiln pottery. The partners produced Rockingham and "yellow queensware" in their "East Liverpool Pottery." During the 1850s and 1860s Knowles and Harvey were best known for their fruit jars (canning jars) and in 1859 they announced that a self-sealing fruit jar had been achieved and that they were seeking a patent. Harvey left the partnership in the mid-1860s but Isaac Knowles continued to operate the pottery, producing self-sealing fruit jars until the early 1870s when glass jars virtually rendered ceramic jars obsolete (WP 28 July 1857, 3 May 1859; Mss. ELMC, Company order sheet 1870; Barber 1893, reprint ed. 1976: 201).

In 1870 Isaac Knowles brought his son Homer S. Knowles and his son-in-law John N. Taylor into the firm. Knowles, Taylor and Knowles continued to manufacture yellow and Rockingham wares but in September 1872 it drew its first kiln of white ware. The commercial success of their ironstone resulted in the abandonment of Rockingham and yellow ware by the following year. By 1877 K.T. & K. had added a new building and increased its capacity to five kilns, which made it the largest pottery in East Liverpool. The firm also fired a glost (glaze) kiln of ironstone ware with natural gas; it claimed to be the first in the world to accomplish this. Knowles, Taylor and Knowles also became one of the first local potteries to establish its own decorating shop and employed Thomas Haden and William Higginson, both skilled English decorators, to manage it. By the end of the decade, K.T.& K. offered ironstone tea sets, dinner services, toilet ware, cooking ware, accessory pieces, and its patented pitchers with britannia lids (ELT 26 August 1876, 18 August 1877; Mss. ELMC, Company price lists 1879; Barber 1893, reprint ed. 1976: 202; McCord 1905: 161).

During the 1880s K.T. & K. prospered under capable and dynamic leadership. The firm was technologically innovative and Isaac Knowles himself is credited with several patents dealing with machinery employed in the industry as well as innovations in the uses of energy. For instance, Knowles' regulated pull-down helped standardize quality in the production of flat ware; this, coupled with increased capital expenditures, assured the growth of the company (Mss. ELMC, United States Patent 1870: #108, 157; McCord 1905: 161).

Knowles, Taylor and Knowles increased its capacity in 1880 with the construction of an eight-kiln plant and the following year purchased the "Buckeye" pottery which it converted to the production of white ironstone. In 1888 K.T. & K. built a new plant for the production of porcelain.

By 1891 Knowles, Taylor and Knowles was incorporated with a capital of $1,000,000, boasted 29 kilns and was the largest pottery in the United States (McCord 1905: 161, 162; Ohio Bureau of Labor Statistics 1895: 35).

Under the supervision of Joshua Poole, former manager of the Belleek factory in Ireland, K. T. & K. produced Belleek ware for a brief period in the late 1880s, but production was halted when the china works burned. When the plant was rebuilt in 1890, K.T. & K. began to produce Lotus Ware. Possessing a fine translucent bone china body, Lotus rivaled European soft-paste porcelains of the period. Catalog sheets and advertisements from the 1890s reveal the wide range of applied and painted decorative motifs on Lotus Ware. Filigree, leaves, flowers, and lace-like patterns were all applied by hand, often producing highly embellished, even lavish, results. Although Lotus was distributed through normal trade channels, it proved too expensive to produce and K.T. & K. discontinued the production of this artificial porcelain around 1897 (Ohio Bureau of Labor Statistics 1895: 35; Mss. ELMC, Company correspondence 5 November

1887, Company catalogs 1889, ca.1894; China, Glass and Lamps 22 January 1896; Garrett 1966: 16–17).

The production of semi-porcelain began in the china works following the discontinuation of Lotus ware. The firm also expanded its lines by adding the production of hotel china, specialties for hospitals and asylums, and, in a separate plant, electrical porcelain. By the early 20th century, Knowles, Taylor and Knowles had more than doubled its capacity of a decade earlier and was offering consumers dinnerware in five shapes and toilet ware in eight shapes (Mss. ELMC, Company price list 1907, Company stationery 1890, Company catalog n.d.).

During this time Joseph Lee, along with Isaac Knowles' younger sons, Willis and Edwin, entered the corporation. Homer Knowles died in 1892 and Isaac retired about the same time. Homer Taylor replaced his father John N. in 1914. The firm continued to operate successfully through this set of managerial changes; however, by the mid-1920s business began to suffer. In 1923 net income for the corporation, including investments, stood at $339,000; by 1926 it had slumped to only $44,850. 29. On 11 March 1929 corporate directors met and approved a motion to join the American Chinaware Corporation stating that ". . . it is for the best interests of this company. . . ." After only two years the American Chinaware Corporation went into receivership and K.T.& K., the largest pottery in the nation for the previous 50 years, ceased all operations (McCord 1905: 162; Calhoun 1922: 68; Mss. ELMC Company Balance Sheet 31 December 1926, Minutes, Board of Directors Meeting 11 March 1929, Bankruptcy Claim #23656 1931).

a

FIGURE 97. Knowles, Taylor and Knowles: a. ironstone ware, 1872–ca. 1878, ware also used by John Wyllie and Son of East Liverpool, 1874–1893, see figure 297a, and William Young and Sons, Trenton, New Jersey, 1870–1879, initials at bottom: "WYS," Barber (1904: 44–45).

FIGURE 97 continued. b. ironstone tableware, 1878–1885, ware; c. ironstone tableware, 1878–1885, ware, size variation of figure 97b and 98a, b, c; d. ironstone hotel ware, 1878–1885, ware, variation of figures 97b, c; 98a, b, c.

FIGURE 98. Knowles, Taylor and Knowles: a. ironstone tableware, 1878–1885, ware, variation of figures 97b, c, d; 98b, c; b. ironstone tableware, 1878–1885, ware, variation of figures 97b, c, d; 98a, c; c. ironstone tableware, 1878–1885, ware, variation of figures 97b, c, d; 98a, b.

FIGURE 99. Knowles, Taylor and Knowles: a. ironstone tablewares, sanitary ware, and "Cable" shape toilet wares, ca. 1885, ware, variation of figures 100a, b; 101a; 99b, c, d, and Coxon & Company, Trenton, New Jersey see Barber (1904: 56); b. ironstone tablewares, sanitary ware, and "Cable" shape toilet wares, ca. 1885, ware, variation of figure 99a, etc.; c. ironstone tablewares, sanitary, ware, and "Cable" shape toilet wares, ca. 1890–ca. 1907, ware variation of figure 99a, etc.; d. ironstone tablewares, sanitary ware, and "Cable" shape toilet wares, ca. 1890–ca. 1907, ware, variation of figure 99a, etc.

a

b

c

d

FIGURE 100. Knowles, Taylor and Knowles: a. ironstone ware, ca. 1881, Barber (1904: 109), variation of figures 99a, b, c, d; 100b; 101a; b. ironstone ware, ca. 1900, Barber (1904: 109), variation of figure 100a; c. ironstone tablewares, ca. 1880–ca. 1890, ware; d. ironstone tablewares, ca. 1880–ca. 1890, ware, variation of figure 100c.

a

b

c

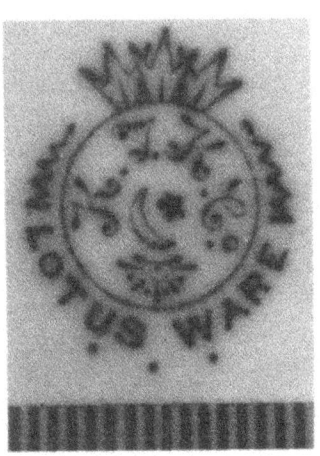

d

FIGURE 101. Knowles, Taylor and Knowles: a. ironstone tableware, ca. 1879, ware, variation of figures 99a, b, c, d; 100a, b; b. Belleek porcelain, 1889, ware; c. bone china, 1891–ca. 1898, ware; d. bone china, 1891–ca. 1898, ware, variation of figure 101c.

FIGURE 102. Knowles, Taylor and Knowles: a. ironstone toilet ware, ca. 1885–ca. 1895, ware, shape name; b. ironstone toilet ware, ca. 1885–ca. 1895, ware, shape name; c. ironstone toilet ware, ca. 1885–ca. 1895, ware, shape name; d. ironstone toilet ware, 1887–ca. 1895, ware, shape name.

FIGURE 103. Knowles, Taylor and Knowles: a. ironstone toilet ware, ca. 1885–ca. 1895, ware, shape name; b. ironstone hotel tableware, ca. 1890, ware, shape name; c. ironstone toilet ware, ca. 1904–ca. 1918, ware, shape name; d. ironstone toilet ware, 1898–1915, ware, shape name.

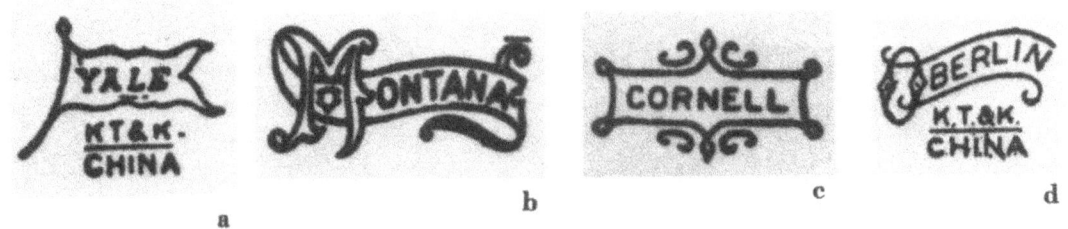

FIGURE 104. Knowles, Taylor and Knowles: a. ironstone and semi-vitreous spittoons, 1905–ca. 1920, Barber (1904: 109), shape name; b. ironstone spittoons, 1905–1906, Barber (1904: 109), shape name; c. ironstone spittoons, 1905–1906, Barber (1904: 109), shape name; d. ironstone spittoons, ca. 1890–1906, Barber (1904: 109), shape name. Other shape names for spittoons include: "Fancy" 1905–1906; "Quincy" 1905–1906; "Rochester" 1905–ca. 1918; "Luna" 1905–ca. 1918.

a   b   c   d

FIGURE 105. Knowles, Taylor and Knowles: a. ironstone table and toilet wares, ca. 1900, Barber (1904: 109); b. iron-stone table and toilet wares, ca. 1900, Barber (1904: 109); c. ironstone table and toilet wares, ca. 1900, Barber (1904: 109); d. ironstone table and toilet wares, ca. 1900, Barber (1904: 109).

a   b

c   d

FIGURE 106. Knowles, Taylor and Knowles: a. ironstone toilet ware, ca. 1904, Barber (1904: 109); b. ironstone table and toilet wares, ca. 1900, Barber (1904: 109); c. ironstone table and toilet wares, ca. 1900, Barber (1904: 109); d. ironstone table and toilet wares, ca. 1900, Barber (1904: 109).

FIGURE 107. Knowles, Taylor and Knowles: a. semi-vitreous hotel, dinnerwares, ca. 1900, ware; b. semi-vitreous toilet and tablewares, 1890–ca. 1905 ware, 1905—used only on underglaze decorations; c. semi-vitreous toilet and dinnerwares, 1900–ca. 1920, ware. Occasionally dinnerware shape or pattern names appear under "K.T. & K. Co." such as: "Ramona" 1907–1915; "Lotus" ca. 1900–ca. 1918; "Plymouth" ca. 1900–1907; "Olympia" ca. 1900; "Ohio" ca. 1900; "Idaho" ca. 1900, "Michigan" ca. 1900; "Orleans" ca. 1900; "Albany" ca. 1900; "St. Louis" 1904–1906; "Portland" 1905 ca. 1910; "America" ca. 1909; "Niana" ca. 1909–ca. 1918; "Tray More" ca. 1909–ca. 1918; "Victory" ca. 1909; "Omar" 1912–1916; "Traymore" 1916–ca. 1918; d. ironstone and semi-vitreous table and toilet ware, (also Lotus Ware), ca. 1890–ca. 1910, ware.

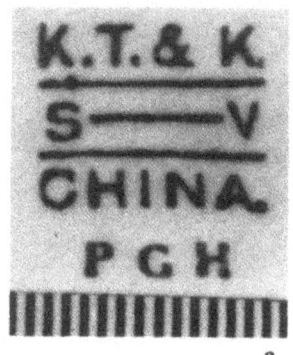

a

b

c

d

FIGURE 108. Knowles, Taylor and Knowles: a. semi-vitreous dinner, toilet, sanitary, and hotel ware, ca. 1905–19 ware; b. semi-vitreous dinnerware, ca. 1925, ware; c. semi-vitreous dinnerware, ca. 1925, ware, variation of Fig 108b; d. semi-vitreous dinnerware, ca. 1925, ware.

FIGURE 109. Knowles, Taylor and Knowles: a. semi-vitreous dinnerware, ca. 1899, ware; b. semi-vitreous hotel ware, ca. 1904, ware; c. semi-vitreous dinnerware, ca. 1920, ware; d. semi-vitreous ware, ca. 1920, ware, variation (not pictured) same style but smaller.

LAUGHLIN BROTHERS (Figure 110a)   1873–1877
HOMER LAUGHLIN CHINA COMPANY (Figures 110–147)   1877–PRESENT

Homer Laughlin came to East Liverpool following the Civil War. In 1868 he began a partnership with Nathaniel Simms for the manufacture of stoneware, but this venture was not successful and Laughlin left the firm soon after its founding. Homer and his brother, Shakespeare, then established a company which sold Rockingham and yellow ware on a wholesale basis. By 1870 the Laughlin Brothers were distributing East Liverpool earthenwares to markets as far away as Massachusetts (McCord 1905: 162; Mss. ELMC, Company order sheet 1870).

In 1873 the city of East Liverpool raised a bonus of $5,000, on a subscription basis, as an inducement for the Laughlin Brothers to construct a $60,000 whiteware plant. Construction of the pottery began in September, and by the Fall of 1874, the plant was in production. The Laughlin Brothers manufactured a fine white ironstone at their "Ohio Valley Pottery" and in 1876 won a premium for their product at the Centennial Exhibition. Later in that same year, the firm introduced a new line of hotel ware. On 21 June 1877, the local newspaper reported that ". . . the partnership between Homer Laughlin and Shakespeare Laughlin, under the firm name of Laughlin Brothers is dissolved by mutual consent." Homer Laughlin continued to operate the "Ohio Valley Pottery" and by 1881 employed almost 150 operatives (East Liverpool Gazette 16 August 1873, 25 August 1874; Mss. ELMC, Company Stationery 1876; ELT 21 June 1877; Columbiana County Directory 1881: 858).

During the 1890s the company added the production of semi-vitreous porcelain and in 1896 Homer Laughlin incorporated his firm as the Homer Laughlin China Company. Two years later, in August 1898, Homer Laughlin retired and moved to California. Control of the corporation passed into the hands of W. E. Wells and a Pittsburgh contingent headed by Marcus Aaron. The firm expanded rapidly under its new management. At the turn of the century, it constructed a second pottery with a 15 kiln capacity, and soon afterward built an additional plant on an adjacent site. By 1905 the growing concern had traded buildings with the National China Company and could boast of three plants with a combined capacity of 36 kilns. Continuing to expand its operation, the Homer Laughlin China Company purchased land across the river from East Liverpool in Newell, West Virginia. By 1914 the firm had built two additional potteries in Newell and the town developed around them. At this time the Laughlin pottery manufactured semi-vitreous dinner, hotel, and toilet wares as well as white granite products (Calhoun 1922: 121; Mss. ELMC, history; Company catalog 1910).

The year 1929 marked the beginning of a new era for the giant pottery producer. Production in the East Liverpool plants was suspended and total operations were shifted to the Newell location which now consisted of five modern, efficient plants, with a capacity of 181 ware kilns and 98 decorating kilns. The tremendous growth in capacity is evidence of the fantastic increase in the demand for inexpensive tablewares during the first quarter of the 20th century. The end of the decade also marked the retirement of W. E. Wells from active management of the firm. Joseph Wells, his son, succeeded him and continued, with the Aarons, to manage the company (Mss. ELMC, Company catalog 1929; Company history).

During the middle decades of the 20th century the Homer Laughlin China Company produced a wide variety (see marks) of dinnerware shapes and patterns as well as oven and kitchen wares. Laughlin lines such as Fiesta, Harlequin, and Eggshell appealed to millions of Americans during the 1930–1960 period. The Homer Laughlin China Company continues to manufacture huge quantities of domestic and commercial wares to the present day. The company still retains its prominent position as one of the largest potteries in the world (China and Glass Trade Directory 1929: 19; Company history).

From 1900 to the present the Homer Laughlin China Company has coded almost all of its production ware. This code includes the month, year, and plant of manufacture (see table 2).

TABLE 2

HOMER LAUGHLIN CHINA COMPANY: WARE DATING SYSTEM
(Courtesy of the Homer Laughlin China Company)

Month	Year	Plant
1900–1909 Number 1–12	Single Number	1, 2, or 3 numbers to designate an East Liverpool plant
1910–1919 Letter	One or two-digit numbers	Letter (and number)
1920–1929 Number	One or two-digit numbers	Letter (and number)
1930–1969 Letter	Two-digit number	Letter (and number)

BEST CHINA BACKSTAMP CODE

Year	Jan	Feb	Mar	Apr	May	June	July	Aug	Sept	Oct	Nov	Dec
1960	—	—	—	—	AE	AF	AG	AH	AI	AJ	AK	AL
1961	BA	BB	BC	BD	BE	BF	BG	BH	BI	BJ	BK	BL
1962	CA	CB	CC	CD	CE	CF	CG	CH	CI	CJ	CK	CL
1963	DA	DB	DC	DD	DE	DF	DG	DH	DI	DJ	DK	DL
1964	EA	EB	EC	ED	EE	EF	EG	EH	EI	EJ	EK	EL
1965	FA	FB	FC	FD	FE	FF	FG	FH	FI	FJ	FK	FL
1966	GA	GB	GC	GD	GE	GF	GG	GH	GI	GJ	GK	GL
1967	HA	HB	HC	HD	HE	HF	HG	HH	HI	HJ	HK	HL
1968	IA	IB	IC	ID	IE	IF	IG	IH	II	IJ	IK	IL
1969	JA	JB	JC	JD	JE	JF	JG	JH	JI	JJ	JK	JL
1970	KA	KB	KC	KD	KE	KF	KG	KH	KI	KJ	KK	KL
1971	LA	LB	LC	LD	LE	LF	LG	LH	LI	LJ	LK	LL
1972	MA	MB	MC	MD	ME	MF	MG	MH	MI	MJ	MK	ML
1973	NA	NB	NC	ND	NE	NF	NG	NH	NI	NJ	NK	NL
1974	OA	OB	OC	OD	OE	OF	OG	OH	OI	OJ	OK	OL
1975	PA	PB	PC	PD	PE	PF	PG	PH	PI	PJ	PK	PL
1976	QA	QB	QC	QD	QE	QF	QG	QH	QI	QJ	QK	QL
1977	RA	RB	RC	RD	RE	RF	RG	RH	RI	RJ	RK	RL
1978	SA	SB	SC	SD	SE	SF	SG	SH	SI	SJ	SK	SL
1979	TA	TB	TC	TD	TE	TF	TG	TH	TI	TJ	TK	TL
1980	UA	UB	UC	UD	UE	UF	UG	UH	UI	UJ	UK	UL
1981	VA	VB	VC	VD	VE	VF	VG	VH	VI	VJ	VK	VL
1982	WA	WB	WC	WD	WE	WF	WG	WH	WI	WJ	WK	WL
1983	XA	XB	XC	XD	XE	XF	XG	XH	XI	XJ	XK	XL
1984	YA	YB	YC	YD	YE	YF	YG	YH	YI	YJ	YK	YL
1985	ZA	ZB	ZC	ZD	ZE	ZF	ZG	ZH	ZI	ZJ	ZK	ZL

FIGURE 110. Laughlin Brothers/Homer Laughlin Pottery: a. ironstone ware, 1873–1877, ware; b. ironstone ware, ca. 1878, ware, shape designation—probably not a production mark, impressed; c. ironstone and porcelain tableware. 1886, ware; d. ironstone tableware, 1886, ware, impressed.

a

b

c

FIGURE 111. Homer Laughlin Pottery: a. ironstone wares, 1877–ca. 1900, ware; b. ironstone wares, 1877–ca. 1900, ware, variation of figure 111a, c; c. ironstone wares, 1877–ca. 1900, ware, variation of figure 111a, b.

FIGURE 112. Homer Laughlin Pottery: a. ironstone wares, 1877–ca. 1900, ware; b. ironstone wares, 1877–ca. 1900, ware, variation of figure 112a, c, d; c. ironstone wares, 1877–ca. 1900, ware, variation of figure 112a, b, d; d. semi-vitreous wares, ca. 1900, ware, variation of Figure 112a, b, c.

FIGURE 113. Homer Laughlin China Company: a. semi-vitreous dinnerware, ca. 1905, ware; b. semi-vitreous dinner-ware, ca. 1907, ware, variation of figure 113a, also "Golden Gate"; c. semi-vitreous Art pottery, ca. 1900, ware.

FIGURE 113 continued. d. semi-vitreous Art pottery, ca. 1900, ware, variation of figure 113c.

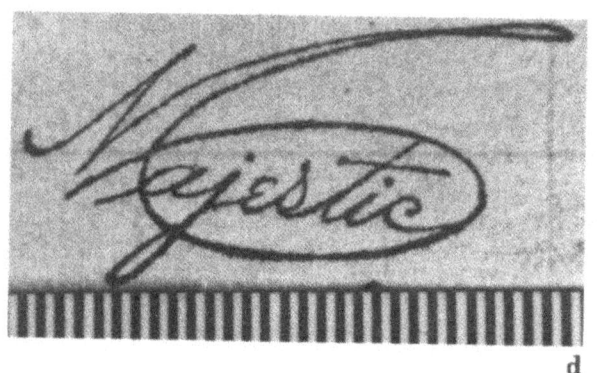

FIGURE 114. Homer Laughlin China Company: a. semi-vitreous art pottery, ca. 1905, ware; b. ironstone hotel ware, ca. 1880–ca. 1900, Barber (1904: 111); c. semi-vitreous tablewares, ca. 1907–ca. 1915, ware, other line name variations include: "Hudson" 1908–ca. 1928; "Angelus" ca. 1909; "Colonial" ca. 1907; "Genesee" ca. 1915; "King Charles" ca. 1915, all in script; "Republic" ca. 1915–ca. 1929, block letters; d. semi-vitreous dinnerware, ca. 1914, Modern Stamp.

a b

c d

FIGURE 115. Homer Laughlin China Company: a. semi-vitreous hotel ware, ca. 1901–ca. 1915, Modern Stamp; b. semi-vitreous hotel ware, ca. 1901–ca. 1915, Modern Stamp; c. semi-vitreous ware, ca. 1901–ca. 1915, Modern Stamp; d. semi-vitreous ware, ca. 1901–ca. 1915, Modern Stamp.

FIGURE 116. Homer Laughlin China Company: a. semi-vitreous ware, 1900–1960 (1919), ware, see company history for explanation of coding system; b. semi-vitreous dinnerware, 1900–1960 (1920), ware, "EMPRESS," ca. 1920–1929; c. semi-vitreous ware, 1900–1960 (1921), ware, hotel ware; d. semi-vitreous ware, 1900–1960 (1926), ware.

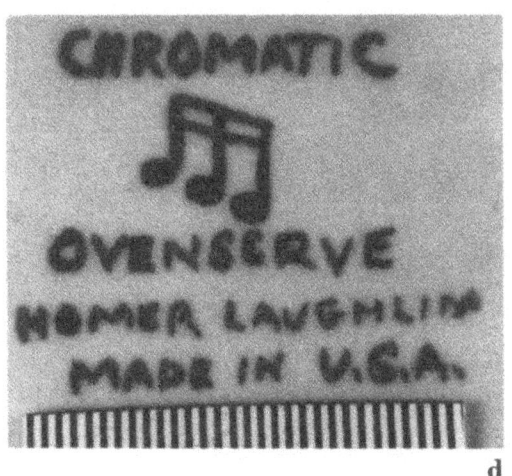

FIGURE 117. Homer Laughlin China Company: a. semi-vitreous ware, 1929–1970, ware; b. semi-vitreous oven ware, ca. 1935–ca. 1950, ware; c. semi-vitreous oven ware, ca. 1935–ca. 1950, ware; d. semi-vitreous oven ware, ca. 1935–ca. 1950, ware.

FIGURE 118. Homer Laughlin China Company: a. semi-vitreous oven ware, ca. 1935, ware, not a line name just open stock; b. semi-vitreous oven ware, 1937–ca. 1945, removable sticker; c. semi-vitreous oven ware, ca. 1935–ca. 1950, ware; d. semi-vitreous oven ware, 1960–present, Quality Stamp.

FIGURE 119. Homer Laughlin China Company: a. semi-vitreous dinnerware, ca. 1941 (1937), ware, see company history for explanation of coding system; b. semi-vitreous dinnerware, ca. 1940 (1938), ware; c. semi-vitreous dinnerware, ca. 1940 (1939), ware; d. semi-vitreous dinnerware, ca. 1940–ca. 1965 (1942), ware.

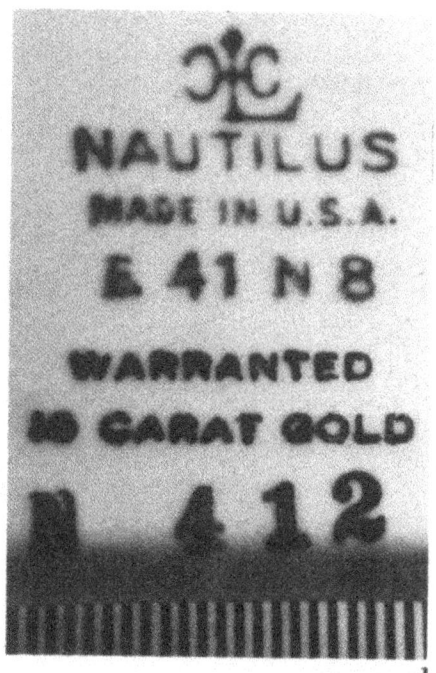

FIGURE 120. Homer Laughlin China Company: a. semi-vitreous dinnerware, ca. 1940–ca. 1955 (1955), ware, see company history for explanation of coding system; b. semi-vitreous dinnerware, ca. 1955, ware; c. semi-vitreous dinnerware, ca. 1941–ca. 1958, ware; d. semi-vitreous dinnerware, ca. 1935–ca. 1950 (1941), ware.

FIGURE 121. Homer Laughlin China Company: a. semi-vitreous dinnerware, ca. 1937–ca. 1957, ware; b. semi-vitreous dinnerware, ca. 1935–ca. 1941, ware; c. semi-vitreous dinnerware, ca. 1935–ca. 1941, ware; d. semi-vitreous ware, ca. 1935, ware.

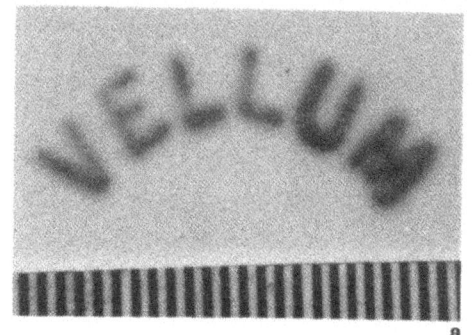

FIGURE 122. Homer Laughlin China Company: a. semi-vitreous dinnerware, ca. 1937–1947, ware; b. semi-vitreous ware, ca. 1936–1947, Quality Stamp; c. semi-vitreous dinnerware, ca. 1939, ware; d. semi-vitreous dinnerware, ca. 1939, ware, mark in color.

FIGURE 123. Homer Laughlin China Company: a. semi-vitreous dinnerware, ca. 1934, ware; b. semi-vitreous dinnerware, ca. 1934, ware; c. semi-vitreous dinnerware, ca. 1935, ware; d. semi-vitreous dinnerware, ca. 1935, ware, mark in color.

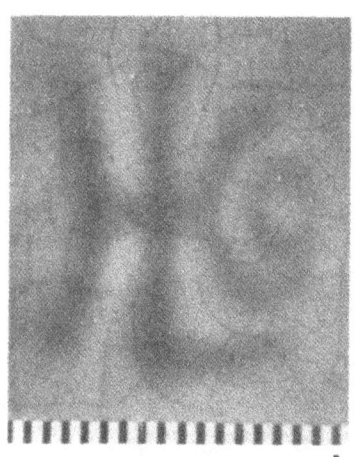

FIGURE 124. Homer Laughlin China Company: a. semi-vitreous ware, ca. 1932, ware, impressed; b. semi-vitreous ware, ca. 1935, ware, impressed; c. semi-vitreous dinnerware, ca. 1940, ware; d. semi-vitreous dinnerware, ca. 1945–ca. 1960, ware.

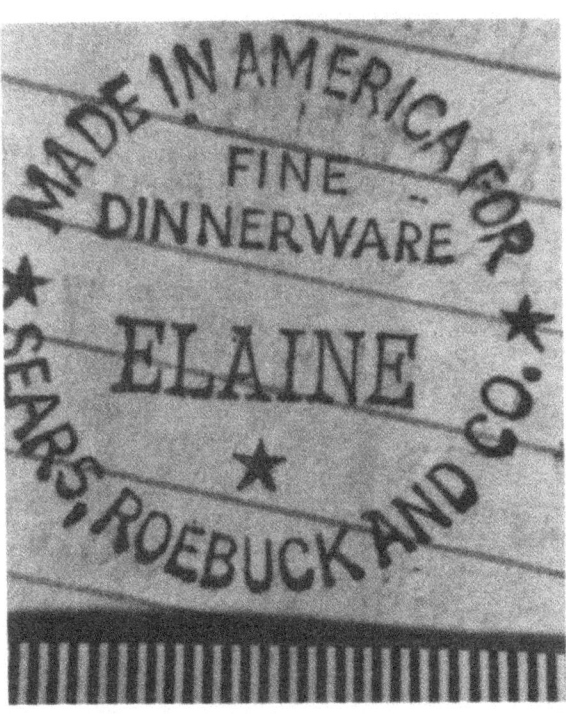

FIGURE 125. Homer Laughlin China Company: a. semi-vitreous dinnerware, 1900–1960 (1945), ware, "Virginia Rose" line ca. 1935–1950; b. semi-vitreous dinnerware, ca. 1936, ware; c. semi-vitreous dinnerware, 1939, company catalog, World's Fair limited edition; d. semi-vitreous dinnerware, 1938–1940, company catalog, also "Nose Gay."

FIGURE 126. Homer Laughlin China Company: a. semi-vitreous dinnerware, 1936–1946, ware, impressed; b. semi-vitreous dinnerware, 1936–1946, ware, impressed, variation of Figure 126a.

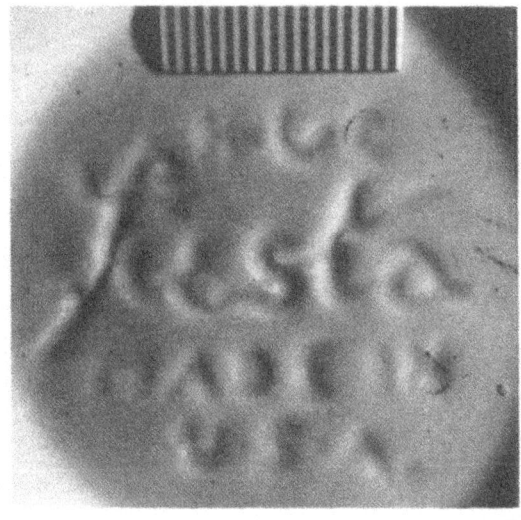

FIGURE 126 continued. c. semi-vitreous dinnerware, 1936–1970, ware, impressed; d. semi-vitreous dinnerware, 1936–1970, ware, impressed.

FIGURE 127. Homer Laughlin China Company: a. semi-vitreous dinnerware, 1936–1970, ware; b. semi-vitreous dinnerware, 1940–1970, ware; c. semi-vitreous dinnerware, 1939–ca. 1943, ware, impressed.

FIGURE 128. Homer Laughlin China Company: a. semi-vitreous dinnerware, ca. 1940–1946, company catalog, also "Neville," "Calais," "Darcy," "Garcon," "Benton" and "Exmoor" patterns; b. semi-vitreous dinnerware, ca. 1940, company catalog, made for Royal Crown Limited, Inc., of Cleveland; c. semi-vitreous dinnerware, ca. 1940–1941, company catalog; d. semi-vitreous dinnerware, 1944, company catalog, special commemorative for Wm. F. Gable Co.

FIGURE 129. Homer Laughlin China Company: a. semi-vitreous oven ware, 1941–ca. 1945, ware; b. semi-vitreous dinnerware, 1941–1950, company catalog; c. semi-vitreous dinnerware, ca. 1940–ca. 1951 (1940), ware; d. semi-vitreous ware, ca. 1940, ware.

FIGURE 130. Homer Laughlin China Company: a. semi-vitreous tableware, ca. 1948, ware, also "Kraft-Pink"; b. semi-vitreous tableware, 1948–ca. 1955, ware; c. semi-vitreous ware, ca. 1949, Company catalog; d. semi-vitreous tableware, ca. 1949, ware, see company history for explanation of coding system.

FIGURE 131. Homer Laughlin China Company: a. semi-vitreous tableware, ca. 1948–ca. 1955, ware; b. semi-vitreous tableware, ca. 1955, ware; c. semi-vitreous children's tableware, ca. 1955, ware; d. semi-vitreous children's tableware, ca. 1955, ware.

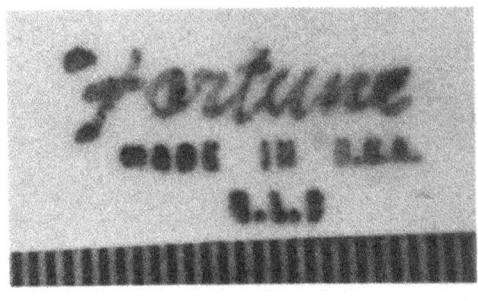

FIGURE 132. Homer Laughlin China Company: a. semi-vitreous dinnerware, ca. 1953–ca. 1960, ware; b. semi-vitreous tableware, 1950–ca. 1960, ware; c. semi-vitreous dinnerware, ca. 1955, ware; d. semi-vitreous dinnerware, 1950–ca. 1960, ware.

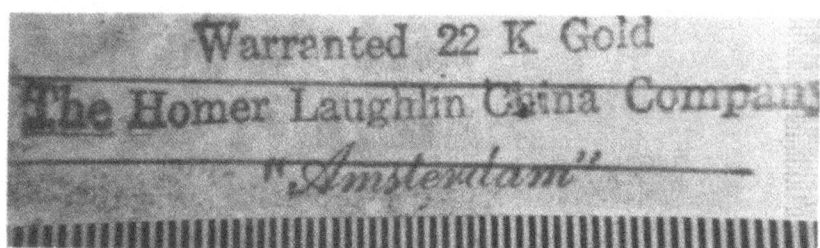

FIGURE 133. Homer Laughlin China Company: a. semi-vitreous ware, ca. 1952, Company records, special for Interstate Utilities Corporation; b. semi-vitreous ware, ca. 1953, Company records, made for Royal Crest Sales Co; c. semi-vitreous ware, ca. 1953, Company records; d. semi-vitreous ware, ca. 1954, ware.

FIGURE 134. Homer Laughlin China Company: a. semi-vitreous dinnerware, ca. 1953–ca. 1960 (1958), ware, see company history for explanation of coding system; b. semi-vitreous dinnerware, ca. 1960, ware; c. semi-vitreous dinnerware, ca. 1960, ware, color mark, also occurs with line names "Snow White," "Cynthia," "June Rose," "Helena" in script under mark; d. semi-vitreous dinnerware, ca. 1960, ware, similar mark Figure 259b.

FIGURE 135. Homer Laughlin China Company: a. semi-vitreous tableware, ca. 1954, ware, see company history for explanation of coding system; b. semi-vitreous dinnerware, ca. 1955, ware, see similar marks Figure 203; c. semi-vitreous ware, ca. 1944, Quality Stamp; d. semi-vitreous dinnerware, ca. 1957, ware.

a

b

c

d

FIGURE 136. Homer Laughlin China Company: a. semi-vitreous table ware, ca. 1955, ware; b. semi-vitreous tableware, ca. 1955, ware, variation of Figure 136a; c. semi-vitreous tableware, ca. 1955, ware; d. semi-vitreous dinnerware, ca. 1955, ware.

FIGURE 137. Homer Laughlin China Company: a. semi-vitreous tableware, ca. 1953, ware; b. semi-vitreous dinner-ware, ca. 1956, ware; c. semi-vitreous ware, ca. 1955, Quality Stamp; d. semi-vitreous ware, ca. 1955, Quality Stamp.

FIGURE 138. Homer Laughlin China Company: a. semi-vitreous ware, ca. 1960, Company records, made for Woolworths; b. semi-vitreous ware, ca. 1960, Company records, special order; c. semi-vitreous ware, ca. 1961, Company records; d. semi-vitreous ware, ca. 1960, ware.

a

b

c

d

FIGURE 139. Homer Laughlin China Company: a. semi-vitreous ware, ca. 1960, Company records, made for Woolworths; b. semi-vitreous ware, ca. 1962, ware; c. semi-vitreous dinnerware, ca. 1964, ware; d. semi-vitreous dinnerware, ca. 1965, ware.

FIGURE 140. Homer Laughlin China Company: a. semi-vitreous ware, ca. 1962, Quality Stamp; b. semi-vitreous ware, ca. 1957, Quality Stamp.

c

d

FIGURE 140 continued. c. semi-vitreous tableware, ca. 1955, ware; d. semi-vitreous dinnerware ca. 1962, ware, dish detergent premium.

FIGURE 141. Homer Laughlin China Company: a. hotel ware, ca. 1973 (1971), ware; b. hotel ware, 1971, Company records; c. semi-vitreous ware, 1970–present, ware; d. semi-vitreous ware, ca. 1975, ware, also "Golden Harvest."

FIGURE 142. Homer Laughlin China Company: a. hotel ware, ca. 1970, ware; b. ca. 1970, ware; c. ca. 1970, ware; d. 1980, ware.

FIGURE 143. Homer Laughlin China Company: a. hotel china, 1960–present (2/1965), ware, see company history for explanation of coding system; b. hotel china, 1960–present (10/1966), ware, variation of Figure 143a; c. hotel china, 1960–present, ware, size variation of Figure 143a; d. hotel china, 1960–present (11/1966), ware.

FIGURE 144. Homer Laughlin China Company: a. semi-vitreous dinnerware, ca. 1977, ware; b. oven ware, ca. 1978, ware; c. semi-vitreous dinnerware, ca. 1935, ware; d. semi-vitreous ware, ca. 1943, Quality Stamp.

FIGURE 145. Homer Laughlin China Company: a. semi-vitreous dinnerware, ca. 1965, Quality Stamp; b. semi-vitreous dinnerware, ca. 1965, Quality Stamp; c. oven ware, ca. 1946–ca. 1960, Quality Stamp; d. ca. 1946–ca. 1960, Quality Stamp.

FIGURE 146. Homer Laughlin China Company: a. hotel ware, post 1946, ware, variation—"Trentwood" not "By/Homer Laughlin"; b. semi-vitreous plate, post 1946, ware; c. ironstone-type dinnerware, ca. 1960, ware; d. vitreous dinnerware, ca. 1962, ware.

FIGURE 147. Homer Laughlin China Company: a. ca. 1965, Quality Stamp; b. dinnerware, ca. 1965, Quality Stamp; c. ironstone-type dinnerware, ca. 1965, Quality Stamp.

THE LIMOGES CHINA COMPANY (Figures 148–161)   1900–1949
THE AMERICAN LIMOGES CHINA COMPANY   1949–1955

The Limoges China Company began operations in 1900 under the name of the Sterling China Company (Figure 148). Organized by Frank and Frederick Sebring, in the new town of Sebring, the firm produced porcelain dinnerware, tea sets, and specialty items such as chocolate, salad, fruit, and soup sets. However, the name was soon changed to the Limoges China Company and it seems that porcelain production was discontinued at this time as only semi-vitreous products were manufactured throughout the rest of the pottery's history. In 1949, as a result of a dispute with the Limoges China Company of France, the name of the firm was officially changed to the American Limoges China Company. The company ceased operations in 1955 (Mss. ELMC, Sterling China Company catalog, n.d.; McKee 1966: 40, 41; China and Glass Trade Directory 1927: 33–52; Mss. ELMC, Limoges China Company stationery 1922; China and Glass Red Book 1949: 17; USPA 1955: 13).

FIGURE 148. Limoges China Company: a. semi-vitreous dinnerware, 1900–ca. 1902, ware; b. semi-vitreous dinnerware, 1900–ca. 1902, ware; c. semi-vitreous dinnerware, 1900–ca. 1902, ware.

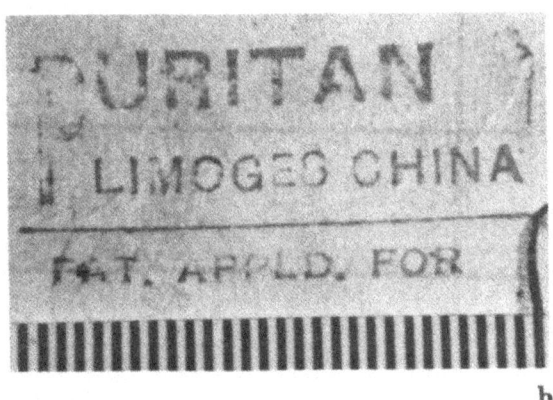

FIGURE 149. Limoges China Company: a. semi-vitreous dinnerware, ca. 1902–ca. 1930, Modern Stamp; b. semi-vitreous dinnerware, ca. 1902–ca. 1910, Modern Stamp; c. semi-vitreous dinnerware, ca. 1910–ca. 1925, Modern Stamp; d. semi-vitreous dinnerware, ca. 1925–ca. 1935, Quality Stamp.

FIGURE 150. Limoges China Company: a. semi-vitreous dinnerware, ca. 1910–ca. 1930, Modern Stamp; b. semi-vitreous dinnerware, ca. 1910–ca. 1930, ware; c. semi-vitreous dinnerware, ca. 1930, ware.

FIGURE 151. Limoges China Company: a. semi-vitreous dinnerware, 1910–ca. 1930, ware; b. semi-vitreous dinnerware, 1910–ca. 1930, Quality Stamp; c. semi-vitreous dinnerware, 1933–1936, Modern Stamp; d. semi-vitreous dinnerware, 1935–1936, ware.

FIGURE 152. Limoges China Company: a. semi-vitreous dinnerware, 1935–1945, Quality Stamp; b. semi-vitreous dinnerware, 1945–ca. 1950, Quality Stamp; c. semi-vitreous dinnerware, 1936–1938, Quality Stamp; d. semi-vitreous dinnerware, 1935–1941, Quality Stamp.

FIGURE 153. Limoges China Company: a. semi-vitreous dinnerware, 1927–1932, Quality Stamp; b. semi-vitreous dinnerware, 1927–1932, Quality Stamp; c. semi-vitreous dinnerware, 1927–1932, Quality Stamp; d. semi-vitreous dinnerware, 1927–1932, ware.

FIGURE 154. Limoges China Company: a. semi-vitreous dinnerware, ca. 1935–1949, ware.

Pattern	Year	Pattern	Year
Arcadia	1948	Lyric	
Blue Daisy	1948	Melody	1948
Bouquet Buds	1948	Monsoon	
Bramble	1948	Nancy Rose	1948
Canterbury	1949	New Princess	1948
Cotillion Pink	1948	Oslo	1949
Chateau	1947	Pompadour Rose	1948
China Rose		Regency Bouquet	1948
Coburg		Rosalie	1947
Easter		Tea Rose	1949
English Rose	1948–1949	Trellis	
Golden Age		Troubadour	
Jenny Lind		Vermillion Rose	1948
LaMarr	1949	Wales	1949
Le Mour		Wheat field	
Lorraine	1948		

FIGURE 155. Limoges China Company: semi-vitreous dinnerware 1939–1948, ware.

Pattern	Year		Pattern	Year
Belvedere			Royal Delight	1948
Blush			Royal Imperial	
Cotillion Pink	1948		Silver Moon	1948
Dogwood	1948		Tea Rose	
Federal Coral pink			Troubadors	1948
Lyceum Blue			White Oats	1948
Orchard	1948			

FIGURES 156. Limoges China Company: a. semi-vitreous dinnerware, 1937–ca. 1950, ware; b. semi-vitreous dinnerware, ca. 1950, ware; c. semi-vitreous dinnerware, 1937–ca. 1950, ware, other pattern names:

Pattern	Year	Pattern	Year
Candle Glow	1948	Prince Rupert	
Commonwealth Rose		Rosalie	
Eleanor	1948	Vermillion Rose	
Lyric Buds	1948	Victoria T	
Maroon Emperor		Wheat Field	1948
Meissen Rosie		White Gold	
National Bouquet		Wood Rose	1948

FIGURE 157. Limoges China Company: a. semi-vitreous dinnerware, ca. 1938, ware; b. semi-vitreous dinnerware, ca. 1942, Quality Stamp; c. semi-vitreous dinnerware, ca. 1942, ware.

a

c

b

FIGURE 158. Limoges China Company: a. semi-vitreous dinnerware, ca. 1928, Quality Stamp; b. semi-vitreous dinnerware, ca. 1930–ca. 1945, Quality Stamp; c. semi-vitreous dinnerware, ca. 1930–ca. 1945, ware.

FIGURE 159. Limoges China Company: a. semi-vitreous dinnerware, ca. 1950, ware; b. semi-vitreous dinnerware, ca. 1950, ware; c. semi-vitreous dinnerware, 1939–ca. 1950, Quality Stamp; d. semi-vitreous dinnerware, 1936–ca. 1950, ware.

FIGURE 160. Limoges China Company: a. semi-vitreous dinnerware, 1949–1955, ware; b. semi-vitreous dinnerware, 1949–1955, ware; c. semi-vitreous dinnerware, 1949–1955, ware; d. semi-vitreous dinnerware, 1949–1955, ware.

FIGURE 161. Limoges China Company: a. semi-vitreous dinnerware, 1946–1949, Quality Stamp; b. semi-vitreous dinnerware, ca. 1939, Quality Stamp; c. semi-vitreous dinnerware, ca. 1950, ware.

McNICOL, BURTON AND COMPANY (Figure 162)   1869–1892

A company composed of Adolph Fritz, William McClure, John McNicol, Patrick McNicol, William Burton Sr., William Burton Jr., and John Dover formed in 1869 and purchased the "Novelty Pottery" from A. J. Marks and Company. The firm, originally named Fritz, McClure and Company became McNicol, Burton and Company when, after only six months, McClure and Fritz withdrew. Extant pieces indicate that this firm produced an excellent Rockingham and yellow ware product. More changes occurred during the 1870s: John Dover retired in 1875, and the following year John McNicol sold his interest to his two sons, H. A. and Daniel Edward. The business was continued under the firm name of McNicol, Burton and Company. Throughout these changes in partnerships, the company continued to expand, adding new buildings and upgrading machinery and equipment. By 1881 it employed 40 workers and produced three kilns of yellow ware and Rockingham per week (Mss. ELMC, Company stationery 1878; Columbiana County Directory 1881: 861; ELT 30 September 1876; Pioneer 1876).

McNicol, Burton and Company continued to operate throughout the 1880s even though William Burton Sr. died in 1881 and his son retired later in the decade. Written documentary evidence is unavailable but examples of white ironstone indicate that the firm added toilet ware and sanitary goods to its line sometime during the 1880s. Following the withdrawal of the Burtons in 1892 the company was incorporated as the D. E. McNicol Pottery Company (Calhoun 1922: 92; Thomas Diary).

FIGURE 162. McNicol, Burton and Company: a. ironstone toilet and sanitary ware, ca. 1885–1892, ware.

FIGURE 162 continued. b. ironstone toilet ware, ca. 1885–1892, ware; c. ironstone toilet ware, ca. 1885–1892, ware.

D. E. McNICOL POTTERY COMPANY (Figures 163–171)   1892–1954

The D. E. McNicol Pottery Company emerged from the former McNicol, Burton and Company in 1892 when Daniel Edward McNicol took over as president and the firm was incorporated. The McNicol pottery produced yellow ware, Rockingham, and a white ironstone it dubbed "semi-granite." In 1902 the firm purchased a second plant which it devoted entirely to Rockingham and yellow wares while it continued to produce ironstone in the original works. The company also built a large pottery at Clarksburg, West Virginia, in 1914 and five years later added a fourth plant in East Liverpool (Calhoun 1922: 93; Vodrey 1945: 284).

During the first quarter of the 20th century, the D. E. McNicol Pottery Company produced hotel, dinner, and toilet wares in semi-granite, semi-porcelain, and c.c. ware. It also continued to manufacture yellow ware products as late as 1927, making it the last firm located in East Liverpool to produce vessels from local clays. The specialties of the McNicol Company, however, were calendar and souvenir plates which were produced in a vast array of styles and decorative motifs. The West Virginia plant specialized in plain white and decorated vitrified china for "Cafes, Clubs, Hotels, Hospitals, Institutions, Railroads, Resaturants, and Steamships" (Mss. ELMC, Company price list 1927, Company catalogs 1914–1927, China and Glass Trade Directory 1927, China, Glass and Lamps 18 November 1896).

In 1928 the D. E. McNicol Pottery Company began to consolidate its operations by disposing of its East Liverpool locations and concentrating on the vitrified china line at the Clarksburg, West Virginia, location. Although ware was produced in the plant during the 1960s, the D. E. McNicol Pottery Company apparently ceased operations in 1954 (USPA 1929: 13, 1954: 12; McKee 1966: 25).

FIGURE 163. D. E. McNicol Pottery Company: a. ironstone tableware, 1892–ca. 1910, ware; b. ironstone tableware, ca. 1900, ware, variation of Figure 163c, d; c. ironstone tableware, ca. 1900, ware, variation of Figure 163b, d; d. ironstone ware, ca. 1900, ware, variation of Figure 163b, c.

FIGURE 164. D. E. McNicol Pottery Company: a. ironstone kitchen and tableware, ca. 1900, ware; b. semi-vitreous ware, ca. 1910, Modern Stamp; c. semi-vitreous dinnerware, ca. 1905, ware; d. semi-vitreous dinnerware, ca. 1905, ware.

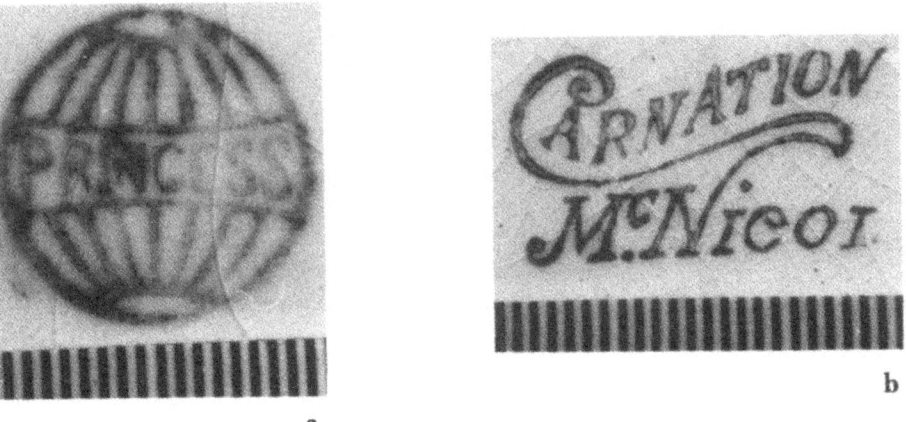

FIGURE 165. D. E. McNicol Pottery Company: a. semi-vitreous dinnerware, 1897–ca. 1915, ware, also "Harvard"; b. semi-vitreous specialty plates (calendar, commemorative, premium, etc), ca. 1902–ca. 1925, ware.

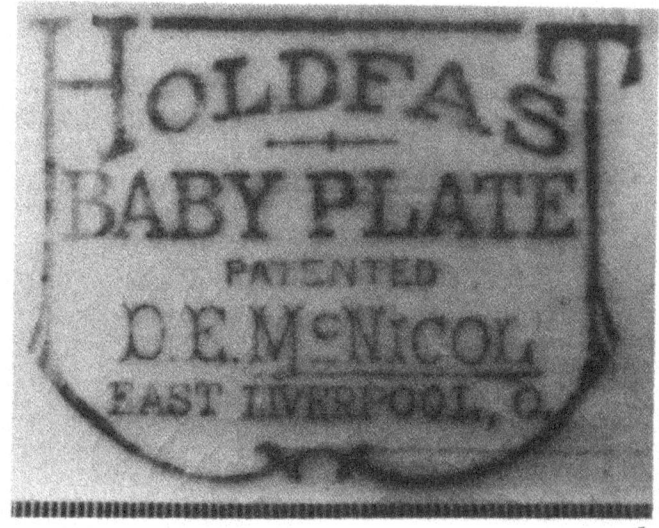

FIGURE 165 continued. c. semi-vitreous baby plates, ca. 1915, ware; d. semi-vitreous baby plates, ca. 1920, ware.

a

b

d

c

FIGURE 166. D. E. McNicol Pottery Company: a. semi-vitreous dinnerware, ca. 1915, ware; b. semi-vitreous dinnerware, ca. 1915–1929, ware; c. semi-vitreous dinnerware, 1914–ca. 1925, ware; d. vitreous hotel china, ca. 1935–ca. 1950, Quality Stamp.

FIGURE 167. D. E. McNicol Pottery Company: a. vitreous institutional (hotel, restaurant, hospital, etc.) ware, 1930–1954, ware. This mark also appears on institutional ware produced during World War II for the United States Quarter Masters Corp "U.S.Q.M.C."; b. vitreous institutional ware, 1930–1954, Quality Stamp , variation of figure 167a, c.; c. vitreous institutional ware, 1930–1954, *American Vitrified China*, published by the American Vitrified China Association, Inc., 1946, variation of figure 167a, b; d. vitreous institutional ware, ca. 1949, Quality Stamp, various names which indicate a color include: "Paragon" ca. 1952; "Rosite"; "Delatone"; "Paladian"; "Pretano."

FIGURE 168. D. E. McNicol Pottery Company: a. vitreous institutional ware, ca. 1933–ca. 1950, Quality Stamp, "John R. Thompson Co." distributors of hotel china; b. vitreous institutional ware, ca. 1933–ca. 1950, Quality Stamp, variation of figure 168a, c, "Albert Pick & Co." and "L. Barth & Co., Inc." distributors of hotel china; c. vitreous institutional ware, ca. 1933–ca. 1950, Quality Stamp, variation of figure 168a, b.; d. vitreous institutional ware, ca. 1935, ware.

FIGURE 169. D. E. McNicol Pottery Company: a. vitreous institutional ware, ca. 1935–1954, Quality Stamp;
b. vitreous institutional ware, ca. 1935–1954, Quality Stamp; c. vitreous institutional ware, ca. 1935–1954, Quality
Stamp; d. vitreous institutional ware, ca. 1935–1954, Quality Stamp.

FIGURE 170. D. E. McNicol Pottery Company: a. vitreous institutional ware, ca. 1935–ca. 1950, Quality Stamp; b. vitreous institutional ware, ca. 1935–ca. 1950, ware; c. vitreous institutional ware, ca. 1935–ca. 1950, Quality Stamp; d. vitreous institutional ware, ca. 1935–ca. 1950, Quality Stamp.

FIGURE 171. D. E. McNicol Pottery Company: a. vitreous institutional ware, ca. 1935–ca. 1950, Quality Stamp; b. vitreous institutional ware, ca. 1935–ca. 1950, Quality Stamp.

T. A. McNICOL POTTERY COMPANY (Figures 172–173)   1913–1929

In 1913 Thomas McNicol, Miles Bennett, and Thomas Cannon established the T. A. McNicol Pottery Company when they purchased the former Globe Pottery. Thomas McNicol was one of four brothers involved in the potteries of East Liverpool during the late 19th and early 20th centuries. The T. A. McNicol Pottery Company manufactured "Semi-vitreous china" dinner and toilet ware specialties in 1915 and by 1917 was also offering cake, berry, fish, and game sets. In a 1921 price list, hotel ware had been added and toilet ware had been eliminated. The firm suspended operations in 1929 (Calhoun 1922: 131; Vodrey 1945: 284; Crockery and Glass Journal 20 December 1917: 187; Mss. ELMC, Company price lists 1915, 1921; USPA 1929: 36).

FIGURE 172. T. A. McNicol Pottery Company: a. semi-vitreous china, 1913–ca. 1925, Modern Stamp; b. semi-vitreous dinnerware, 1915–1929 (1922), ware; c. semi-vitreous dinnerware, ca. 1924 (1927), ware.

FIGURE 173. T. A. McNicol Pottery Company: a. semi-vitreous china, ca. 1924 (1926), Modern Stamp; b. semi-vitreous dinnerware, ca. 1924, ware.

McNICOL-SMITH COMPANY (Figures 174–175)   1889–1907
McNICOL-CORNS CHINA COMPANY (Figure 176a, b, c)   1907–1928
CORNS CHINA COMPANY (Figure 176d)   1928–1932

William Smith and D. E. McNicol purchased the old Baum pottery at Wellsville, Ohio, in 1899 and began to develop it for the production of semi-porcelain. The firm of McNicol and Smith operated the pottery until 1907 when Smith departed to look after his interests in Taylor, Smith and Taylor. A. W. Corns filled Smith's place and the name of the company became the McNicol-Corns China Company. The new firm also produced semi-porcelain dinnerware in its 10 kiln plant. McNicol retired from the business in 1928 but Corns continued to operate the plant, producing dinnerware and adding toilet and hotel ware. A fire destroyed the plant in 1932, after which Corns distributed the warehouse stock through the China Specialty Company of Wellsville (Calhoun 1922: 154; Vodrey 1945: 287; Barth v. 1 1926: 399; China and Glass Directory 1933: 44).

FIGURE 174. McNicol-Smith Company: a. ironstone toilet ware, 1889–ca. 1901, ware; b. ironstone tableware, 1889, ca. 1901, ware, variation of Figure 174c, d; c. semi-vitreous tableware, ca. 1895–1907, ware, variation of Figure 174b; d. semi-vitreous tableware, ca. 1903, ware, variation of Figure 174b, c.

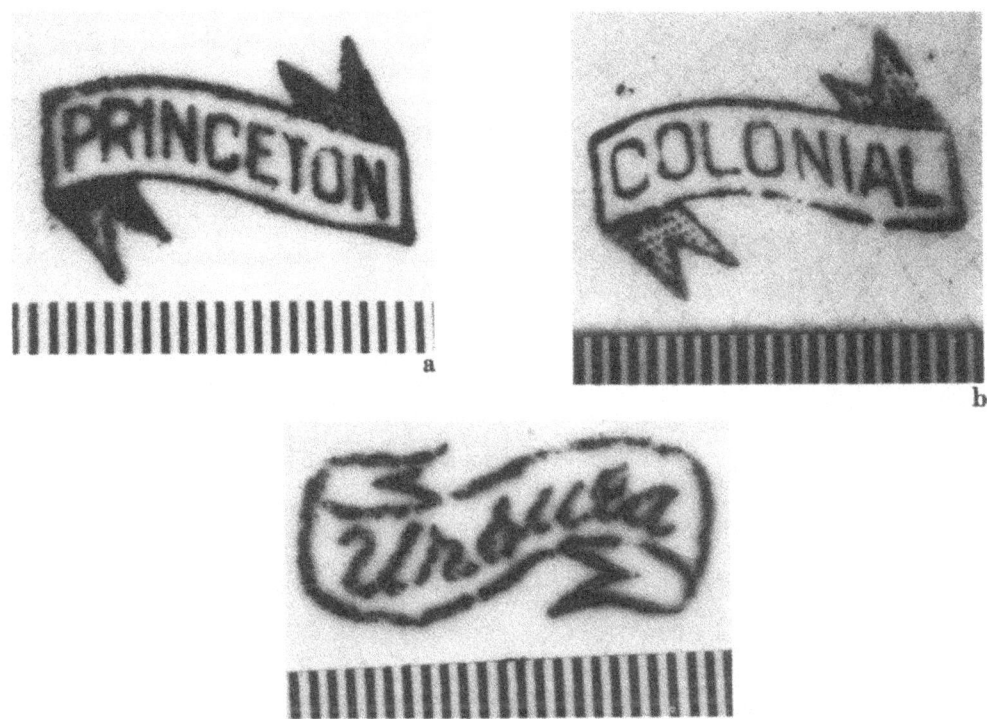

FIGURE 175. McNicol-Smith Company: a. semi-vitreous ware, 1900–1907, ware, variation of Figure 175b; b. semi-vitreous ware, 1900–1907, ware, variation of Figure 175a; c. semi-vitreous ware, 1900–1907, ware.

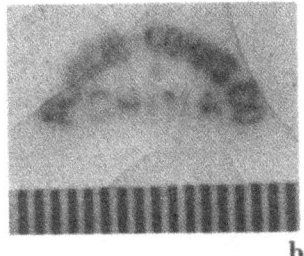

FIGURE 176. McNicol-Corns China Company/Corns China Company: a. semi-vitreous tableware, 1907–1928, ware; b. semi-vitreous tableware, 1907–1928, ware.

FIGURE 176 continued. c. semi-vitreous tableware, 1907–1928, ware; d. semi-vitreous kitchenware, 1928–1932, ware.

MORLEY ASSOCIATIONS (Figures 177–178)   1878–1891
PIONEER POTTERY COMPANY (Figures 179–180)   1884–1900

George Morley, a Staffordshire potter, arrived in East Liverpool around 1852 and worked for several local potteries prior to his partnership with James Godwin and William Flentke (see history). These men operated the ''Salamander Pottery Works'' from 1855 to 1878 when Morley withdrew from the partnership. In partnership with Harmer Michaels and I. B. Clark, Morley organized a company and constructed a two kiln pottery in nearby Wellsville, Ohio. In July 1879 the firm began operations with 60 employees (Pioneer 1876; McCord 1905: 173).

Morley and Company, as the firm was known, produced ironstone china and ''American Majolica'' in its new plant. In addition to traditional ironstone dinner and toilet wares, the colorful majolica was offered in such pieces as pitchers in the forms of a fish or an owl, napkin plates, and highly decorated jugs, compotes, and accessory dishes (Mss. ELMC, Company catalog sheet n.d.).

In April 1884 the partnership was dissolved by ''. . . limitation and mutual consent . . .'' when Morley sold his interests to the others. Clark and Michaels continued to operate the ''Pioneer Pottery Works'' producing plain and decorated ironstone tea, dinner, and toilet sets until 1890 when the firm went into receivership. In 1896 a new Pioneer Pottery Company emerged which produced semi-porcelain; however, this new enterprise did not survive for any significant length of time. Clark continued to operate the ''Pioneer Pottery'' intermittently until 1900 (Barber 1904, reprint ed. 1976: 128). The pottery changed hands shortly after this and became the Wellsville China Company (ELT 19 April 1884; Mss. ELMC, unidentified advertisement August 1889; McCord 1905: 173).

Upon his return to East Liverpool from Wellsville in 1884, Morley and his two sons purchased the ''Lincoln Pottery'' from West, Hardwick and Company. The new firm, known as George Morley and Sons, also produced ironstone china and majolica. In October 1891 the company declared bankruptcy and the court ordered that all of the assets be sold in order to pay the company's debts (ELT 7 June 1884; The Evening Review 29 October 1891).

FIGURE 177. Morley and Company: a. ironstone ware, 1879–1884, ware; b. ironstone ware, 1879–1884, ware; c. ironstone (majolica) ware, 1879–1884, ware, note misspelling of majolica; d. ironstone (majolica) ware, 1879–1884, ware, variation of Figure 177c.

FIGURE 178. George Morley and Sons: a. ironstone tablewares, 1884–1891, ware; b. ironstone tableware, 1884–1891, ware; c. ironstone (majolica) ware, 1884–1891, ware.

FIGURE 179. Pioneer Pottery Company (Wellsville): a. ironstone table and toilet ware, 1884–ca. 1891, ware; b. ironstone table and toilet ware, 1884–ca. 1891, ware; c. ironstone toilet wares, 1884–ca. 1890, ware.

a

b

c

d

FIGURE 180. Pioneer Pottery Company (Wellsville): a. porcelain ware, 1884–ca. 1890, Barber (1904: 128); b. iron-stone ware, 1884–ca. 1890, Barber (1904: 128); c. semi-porcelain tableware, 1896–1900, ware; d. semi-porcelain tableware, 1896–1900, ware.

MOUNTFORD AND COMPANY (Figure 181)   1891–1897

There is little information currently available concerning this firm, however, enough fragments exist to construct a skeletal history.

In 1882 John Rowe, Thomas Robinson, John Mountford, Edward Owens, and Ambrose Massey formed a company and took over the "Diamond Stilt Works" previously operated by Robinson and Company. An 1887 county business review lists a company called Rowe and Mountford which employed 20 people and produced stilts, pins, spurs, and other potter's supplies. Although some of these supplies were made within local potteries for their own use, the majority were imported from England (Calhoun 1922: 133; Annual Business Review of Columbiana County 1887: 26).

The firm of Rowe and Mountford was dissolved in September 1891. The local newspaper reported that Rowe was leaving the company following arguments that resulted in blows. It is conceivable that the arguments focused on a decision to produce pottery, for it was also in 1891 that white granite wares were added to the company's line. By 1893, the firm was known as Mountford and Company and was manufacturing white granite and decorated ware. There is no record of the continued production of potter's supplies, and Mountford and Company sold out to George Murphy in 1897 (The Daily Crisis 29 September 1891; Vodrey 1945: 286; Mss. ELMC, Company stationery 1893; The Daily Crisis 23 February 1897).

FIGURE 181. Mountford and Company: a. ironstone ware, 1891–1897, company letterhead; b. ironstone ware, 1891–1897, ware.

GEORGE C. MURPHY POTTERY COMPANY (Figure 182)   1897–1901/1903–1904

George C. Murphy was an entrepreneur who invested his money in a pottery concern without having had any practical experience as a potter himself. Murphy, who came to East Liverpool in 1874, began a retail clothing business in 1889. In 1897 he organized the George C. Murphy Pottery Company and purchased the old Rowe and Mountford building. By November of that year, the firm was offering semi-vitreous dinnerware, vitreous hotel china, and ironstone toilet sets. The Murphy company joined the short-lived East Liverpool Potteries Company in 1901. George Murphy served as president of the conglomerate for a year and a half, but when the organization faltered in 1903, he pulled out and began operations again as an independent. In April 1904 the plant was destroyed by fire and was never rebuilt (McCord 1905: 644; Illustrated Glass and Pottery World November 1897, March 1898).

FIGURE 182. George C. Murphy Pottery Company: a. vitreous hotel china, 1897–1901, Barber (1904: 114); b. semi-vitreous or ironstone ware, 1897–1901, Barber (1904: 114); c. ironstone toiletware, 1897–1901, ware; d. semi-vitreous tableware, 1897–1901, ware.

NATIONAL CHINA COMPANY (Figures 183–187)   1899–1929

The National China Company, formed in 1899 by Thomas Fischer, S. C. Williams, Samuel Larkins, J. H. Warner and John Stamm, built a modern pottery in East Liverpool's East End section. Production operations began at the plant in 1900. The firm produced ironstone and semi-porcelain dinner and toilet wares as well as specialty items at this pottery until 1903 when it traded plants with the Homer Laughlin China Company (Mss. ELMC, Company stationery 1911; Calhoun 1922: 130).

In 1911, after only eight years, the National China Company sold its East Liverpool plant to the Harker Pottery Company and transferred operations to nearby Salineville, Ohio. Here the firm enjoyed a great deal of success with a line of hotel ware, two shapes of toilet ware, and at least three different shapes in its dinnerware line. As early as 1918, they introduced the "La Rosa" pattern dinner service which apparently became very popular; by 1923 it was the only line in dinnerware the company offered (USPA 1911: 14; Mss. ELMC, Company price lists n.d., 1923; Crockery and Glass Journal 19 December 1918: 205).

The National China Company joined the American Chinaware Corporation in 1929. This effort at consolidating some of the area's most prominent potteries was futile. The corporation went into receivership and declared bankruptcy in 1931 (for more information see American Chinaware Corporation) (Mss. ELMC, Engineering report 1929, Bankruptcy claim #23656, 1931).

FIGURE 183. National China Company: a. semi-vitreous tableware, 1899–1911, ware; b. semi-vitreous specialty ware, 1899–1911, ware; c. semi-vitreous dinnerware, 1899–1911, ware; d. ironstone (hotel) sanitary ware, 1899–1911, ware.

FIGURE 184. National China Company: a. semi-vitreous dinnerware, 1899–1911, ware; b. semi-vitreous dinnerware, 1899–1911, ware; c. semi-vitreous dinnerware, 1911–1929, Modern Stamp, also "Ivory" and "La Rosa"; d. semi-vitreous dinnerware, 1911–ca. 1923, ware.

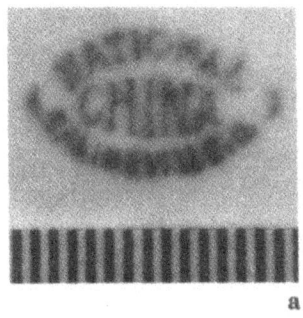

FIGURE 185. National China Company: a. semi-vitreous dinnerware, 1911–1929, ware; b. ironstone toiletware, 1911–ca. 1924, Modern Stamp; c. unknown type, 1911–1929, certificate for American Chinaware Corporation; d. unknown type, 1911–1939, certificate for American Chinaware Corporation.

FIGURE 186. National China Company: a. ironstone dinnerware and toiletware, 1911–ca. 1924, ware; b. semi-vitreous decorative flatware, 1911–ca. 1924, ware.

FIGURE 186 continued. c. semi-vitreous ware, 1911–ca. 1924, company catalog, variation of Figure 186b.

FIGURE 187. National China Company: a. semi-vitreous dinnerware, 1925–1929, (1928) certificate for American Chinaware Corporation; b. unknown type hotel, dinner and toilet ware, 1911–ca. 1924, company catalog; c. semi-vitreous hotel ware, 1911–ca. 1924, company catalog; d. unknown type hotel ware, 1911–ca. 1924, company catalog, also with "ELO" beneath "Hotel."

OLIVER CHINA COMPANY (Figure 188)   1899–circa 1908

The Oliver China Company began operations in Sebring, Ohio, in 1899. It was the first pottery in the town newly founded by the Sebrings and was operated by George E. Sebring. The Oliver China Company manufactured semi-vitreous toilet and tablewares. Around 1908 George Sebring sold the company to his bother Ellsworth H. and the name was changed to the E. H. Sebring China Company. This company continued to produce semi-porcelain (McKee 1966: 40, 41).

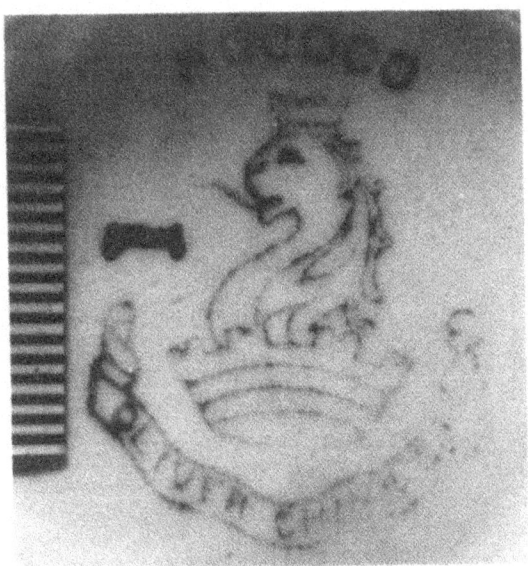

FIGURE 188. Oliver China Company: a. semi-vitreous table and specialty wares, 1899, ware; b. semi-vitreous table and toilet wares, 1899–ca. 1908, ware; c. semi-vitreous table and toilet wares, 1899–ca. 1908, Barber (1904: 136); d. semi-vitreous specialty wares, ca. 1900, ware.

JOHN PATTERSON AND SONS POTTERY COMPANY (Figure 189)   1883–1900
PATTERSON BROTHERS COMPANY   1900–1907

The John Patterson and Sons Pottery began producing yellow and Rockingham wares in 1883 at a plant in Wellsville, Ohio. The pottery boasted four kilns and operated without a change in management until 1900 when the sons took control. In 1907 the pottery was offered for sale and in 1917 became the first plant of the Sterling China Company. Pieces at the East Liverpool Museum of Ceramics attributed to Patterson include mugs, a soap dish, a humidor, pitchers, nappies, bowls, and a teapot. All of the examples are plain with little modeling (McCord 1905: 173; Vodrey 1945: 287; Glass and Pottery World 1907: 27).

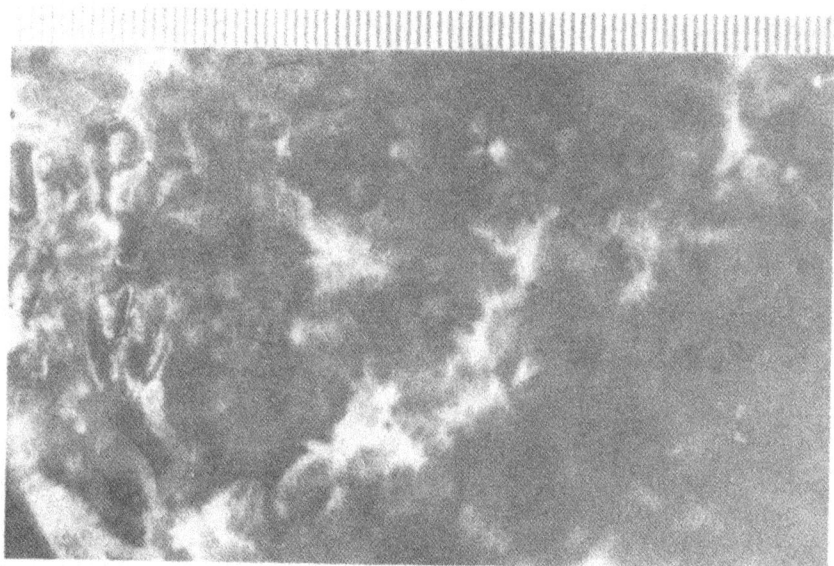

FIGURE 189. John Patterson and Sons: Rockingham ware, 1883–1900, ware, impressed mark reads "J. Pattersons/ Wellsville/Ohio."

PIONEER POTTERY COMPANY (Figure 190)   1935–PRESENT

In 1935, Grant Stover, George Singer, and Albert Pelley purchased the Hall China Company's No. 3 plant. From 1935 to 1958, the Pioneer Pottery Company produced florist ware, tea sets, and artwares. These wares were distributed through Singer's and Stover's "Pearl China and Pottery Company" (see history) as well as larger chain department stores. In 1958, Pioneer was sold to the Craftmaster Corporation of Toledo, Ohio. General Mills purchased Craftmaster in 1968 and in 1973 sold the plant to Lawrence Howell, an employee. At present, Howell, his wife Mary, and their daughter and son-in-law, Arlene and William Bickle, own and operate the business (Jack Hall 1981, pers. comm.; Crockery and Glass Red Book 1945: 40; company information 1981).

FIGURE 190. Pioneer Pottery Company (East Liverpool): semi-vitreous novelty and table wares, 1935–1958, ware, present mark: Connestoga Wagon with "Pioneer" on canvas cover not included because of photographic error.

POTTER'S CO-OPERATIVE COMPANY (Figures 191–199)   1882–1925

The Potter's Co-operative Company began operations in 1882 as a direct result of a management/labor conflict in East Liverpool. Operatives were attempting to organize under the auspices of the Knights of Labor, and the management of eight local potteries banded together and refused to allow participating employees to work (ELT 20 January 1883, 17 February 1883). A group of these potters joined together and formed this co-operative company (Company stock ledger 1882). The new firm, headed by H. A. McNicol, purchased the "Dresden Pottery Works" from Brunt, Bloor, Martin and Company.

The firm produced ironstone toilet sets, dinnerware, tea sets, sanitary ware, and vitreous hotel china. In 1890 the company added semi-porcelain to its growing line (Mss. ELMC, Company catalogs ca. 1895, 1918, ca. 1925; Vodrey 1945: 284).

The joint stock company aspect of the new firm did not last long. After only a year some of the operative stockholders, feeling that they were being discriminated against, initiated legal proceedings against other members of the firm. These internal problems led to the demise of the co-operative aspect. Following reorganization, H. A. McNicol remained as president of the firm until his death, after which his son Harry assumed control (Barth 1926: 210).

The Potter's Co-operative operated until 1925 when a new corporation, the Dresden Pottery Company, purchased the "Dresden Pottery Works" (Mss. ELMC, Articles of Incorporation—Dresden Pottery Company 1925).

FIGURE 191. Potter's Co-operative Company: a. ironstone table and toilet ware, 1882–ca. 1895, ware; b. ironstone table and toilet ware, 1882–ca. 1895, ware, variation of Figure 191a, c, d; c. ironstone table and toilet ware, 1882–ca. 1895 (1890), ware, variation of Figure 191a, b, d; d. ironstone table and toilet ware, ca. 1892, ware, variation of Figure 191a, b, c.

FIGURE 192. Potter's Co-operative Company: a. ironstone toilet ware, ca. 1896, ware; b. ironstone toilet ware, ca. 1896, ware, variation of Figure 192a; c. ironstone toilet ware, ca. 1896, company advertisement; d. ironstone toilet ware, ca. 1896, ware, variation of Figure 192c.

FIGURE 193. Potter's Co-operative Company: a. ironstone table and toilet ware, ca. 1896, ware; b. ironstone table and toilet ware, ca. 1895, ware, variation of Figure 193a; c. ironstone toilet and specialty ware, 1897, ware; d. ironstone table ware, ca. 1885–1895, ware.

FIGURE 194. Potter's Co-operative Company: a. vitreous hotel ware, ca. 1896, company advertisement; b. ironstone tableware, ca. 1900, ware; c. ironstone tableware, 1890–ca. 1900, ware; d. ironstone table and sanitary ware, ca. 1897, ware.

FIGURE 195. Potter's Co-operative Company: a. hotel ware, ca. 1896, company advertisement; b. hotel ware, ca. 1904, ware, impressed; c. hotel ware, ca. 1904, ware, impressed, variation of Figure 195b; d. hotel ware, ca. 1910, ware, variation of Figure 195a.

FIGURE 196. Potter's Co-operative Company: a. ironstone tableware, 1890–ca. 1900, ware; b. ironstone ware, ca. 1905, Barber (1904: 112); c. semi-vitreous table and toilet ware, ca. 1895–ca. 1910, ware, variation of Figure 196b, d; d. semi-vitreous table and toilet ware, ca. 1915, ware, variation of Figure 196b, c.

FIGURE 197. Potter's Co-operative Company: a. semi-vitreous specialty ware, ca. 1914. ware; b. semi-vitreous dinnerware, ca. 1908–ca. 1915, ware; c. semi-vitreous tableware, ca. 1915, ware.

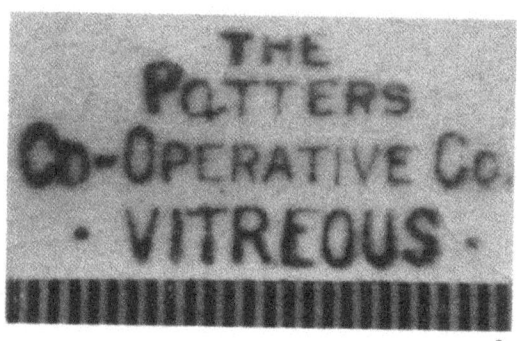

FIGURE 198. Potter's Co-operative Company: a. vitreous ware, ca. 1915, Modern Stamp; b. vitreous ware, ca. 1915, ware, variation of Figure 197c.

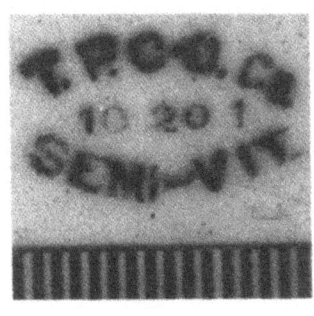

FIGURE 199. Potter's Co-operative Company: a. semi-vitreous tableware, ca. 1920, ware; b. semi-vitreous tableware, ca. 1920 (1922), ware; c. semi-vitreous tableware, ca. 1920–1925, ware, pattern name included; d. semi-vitreous tableware, ca. 1923 (1925), ware, transitional mark—see Dresden Pottery Company.

ROYAL CHINA COMPANY (Figures 200–208)   1933–PRESENT

   The Royal China Company succeeded the E. H. Sebring China Company in 1933 when it purchased the latter's plant. The structure had been abandoned for several years following the collapse of The American Chinaware Corporation but by 1939 the firm had remodeled the plant and employed 713 workers. The Royal China Company produced semi-vitreous dinnerware, baking and cooking ware, tea sets, premium assortments, and art ware. In 1969 the firm was purchased by the Jeanette Glass Corporation, under whose ownership it operates to the present day (McKee 1966: 40; East Liverpool Review 1 February 1937; China and Glass Red Book 1946: 52; Company information 1981).

a

c

b

FIGURE 200. Royal China Company: a. semi-vitreous dinnerware, ca. 1934–ca. 1960, ware; b. semi-vitreous dinnerware, 1934–ca. 1960 (1953), ware; c. semi-vitreous dinnerware, 1934–ca. 1960, Quality Stamp.

FIGURE 200 continued. d. oven ware, 1938–1951, Quality Stamp.

FIGURE 201. Royal China Company: a. semi-vitreous dinnerware, ca. 1940–ca. 1950, Quality Stamp.

FIGURE 201 continued: b. semi-vitreous serving ware, ca. 1940–ca. 1950, ware; c. semi-vitreous dinnerware, ca. 1940–ca. 1950, Quality Stamp; d. semi-vitreous dinnerware, ca. 1940–ca. 1950, ware.

FIGURE 202. Royal China Company: a. semi-vitreous serving ware, 1934–ca. 1960, ware; b. semi-vitreous dinnerware, ca. 1940–ca. 1950, Quality Stamp.

FIGURE 203. Royal China Company (see similar mark Figure 136b): a. semi-vitreous dinnerware, ca. 1950–ca. 1960 (1956), ware; b. semi-vitreous dinnerware, ca. 1950–ca. 1960, ware; c. semi-vitreous decorative flatware, ca. 1950–ca. 1960, ware, other pattern names "Pink Tradition" and "Camelot."

FIGURE 204. Royal China Company: a. semi-vitreous dinnerware, 1949–ca. 1960 (1956), ware: b. semi-vitreous dinnerware, 1949–ca. 1960, ware; c. semi-vitreous dinnerware, 1951–ca. 1960, ware.

FIGURE 205. Royal China Company: a. semi-vitreous dinnerware, 1934–1955, ware; b. semi-vitreous dinnerware, ca. 1940–1955, Quality Stamp; c. semi-vitreous dinnerware, ca. 1940–1955, Quality Stamp; d. semi-vitreous dinnerware, 1934–1960, Modern Stamp.

FIGURE 206. Royal China Company: a. semi-vitreous dinnerware, 1950–ca. 1955 (1950), ware; b. semi-vitreous dinnerware, 1952–ca. 1955, ware; c. semi-vitreous dinnerware, 1951–ca. 1960 (1953), ware; d. semi-vitreous dinnerware, 1951–ca. 1960 (1956), ware.

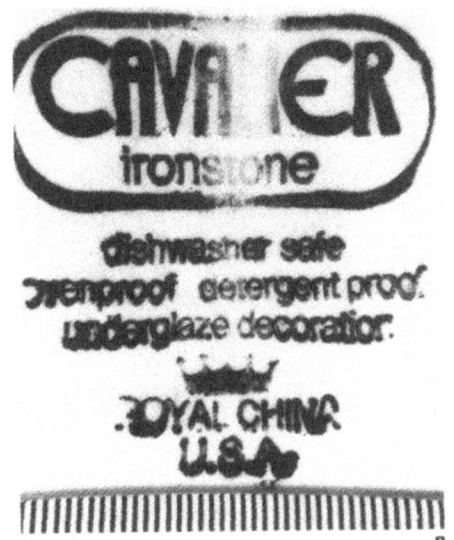

FIGURE 207. Royal China Company: a. ironstone-type dinnerware, ca. 1968, ware, (East Palestine plant).; b. ironstone-type dinnerware, ca. 1968, ware; c. ironstone-type dinnerware, ca. 1968, ware; d. semi-vitreous dinnerware, ca. 1970, ware.

FIGURE 208. Royal China Company: a. ironstone-type dinnerware, ca. 1968, ware, (East Palestine plant); b. iron-stone-type dinnerware, ca. 1968, ware; c. semi-vitreous dinnerware, ca. 1970, ware; d. semi-vitreous dinnerware, 1969–present, ware.

SAXON CHINA COMPANY (Figure 209)   1911–1929
FRENCH-SAXON CHINA COMPANY (Figure 210)   1935–1964

The Saxon China Company began operations in 1911 in Sebring, Ohio, under the direction of Fred Sebring (see Sebring Pottery Company). In 1916 he sold the plant to his brother, O. H. Sebring, who operated the Saxon China Company under the Sebring Manufacturing Company, a holding company, until 1929. Saxon also embraced the French China Company and the Strong Manufacturing Company. The firm manufactured plain and decorated semi-vitreous dinnerware. Operations at the plant were suspended around 1931 when the holding company, which had joined the American Chinaware Corporation in 1929, went bankrupt along with the rest of the member firms (USPA 1911: 14; McKee 1966: 41; China and Glass Trade Directory 1927: 33–52; Mss. ELMC, Company purchase order 1924, American Chinaware Corporation, Records of Formation 1929, Bankruptcy Claim #23656 1931).

Following the disbandment of the American Chinaware Corporation, W. V. Oliver purchased the former Saxon plant and began operations as the French-Saxon China Company by May 1935. In 1936 the firm offered semi-porcelain dinnerware and tea sets. Oliver died in 1963 and the Royal China Company acquired the company's capital stock in 1964 (USPA 1936: 13; China and Glass Directory 1936; McKee 1966: 44; USPA 1965: 9).

FIGURE 209. Saxon China Company: a. ironstone-type dinnerware, 1911–ca. 1920, ware; b. semi-vitreous ware, ca. 1920, Modern Stamp; c. semi-vitreous ware, ca. 1925, Modern Stamp.

FIGURE 210. French-Saxon China Company: a. semi-vitreous tableware, 1935–1964, company advertisement, also "Star Flower," "The Haviland," "Breeze"; b. semi-vitreous ware, ca. 1945, Quality Stamp; c. semi-vitreous dinnerware, ca. 1940–ca. 1958, ware.

SEBRING POTTERY COMPANY (Figures 211–218)   1887–1940 (1948)

The Sebring Pottery Company was formed in 1887 when the five Sebring brothers (George E., Oliver, Ellsworth H., Frank A., Joseph) formed a partnership with George Ashbaugh and Sampson Turnbull. The Sebring brothers were the sons of George A. Sebring who had worked in several East Liverpool potteries. The newly formed partnership purchased the former Agner and Gaston pottery in 1887. The idle yellow ware plant had to be repaired and much of the out-dated machinery needed to be replaced before the production of white granite could begin. About two years later the Sebring brothers purchased the interests of their former partners and continued production on their own (McCord 1905: 172).

During the 1890s the Sebring brothers added three potteries to their holdings and expanded their production to include "semi-vitreous porcelain." In 1893 the Sebrings leased the plant of the former East Palestine Pottery Company and three years later built the Ohio China Company, also in East Palestine, Ohio. The four Sebring brothers (Joseph was killed in 1890) gave up their lease in East Palestine in 1898 and built a six kiln pottery in East Liverpool's East End. The new pottery (see French China Company), called "Klondyke" because of its great distance from the center of town, attracted workers to the area and a small community sprang up. During the 1890s the Sebring Pottery Company produced plain and decorated semi-porcelain and ironstone dinner and toilet sets, commemorative plates, and accessory pieces (Illustrated Glass and Pottery World December 1896, October 1897, May 1898; Mss. ELMC, Company catalog sheets 1898, Company stationery 1896).

Seeking room to expand their potteries and to increase their total operation, the Sebring brothers purchased 2,000 acres of land in Mahoning County, Ohio, in 1898. The following year they laid out the town of Sebring. In addition to moving their two East Liverpool firms to Sebring, the brothers established several other potteries in the town during the early 20th century, including the Oliver China Company, the Strong Manufacturing Company, the Limoges China Company, the Saxon China Company, the E. H. Sebring China Company and the Sebring China Company. During the early decades of the 20th century, the Sebring pottery interests experienced many changes in management and organization utilizing a confusing array of holding companies and corporate entities such as Crescent China and Leigh China of Alliance, Ohio. Throughout these changes the Sebring-owned potteries continued to produce a good quality semi-vitreous dinnerware.

In 1940 the company was absorbed by The Limoges China Company. Limoges continued using the Sebring China line until 1948 (McCord 1905: 172, 173; Calhoun 1922: 129; McKee 1966: 39; China and Glass Directory 1941: 42, 1948: 44).

FIGURE 211. Sebring Pottery Company: a. ironstone table and toilet wares, 1887–1900, ware; b. ironstone table and toilet wares, 1887–1900, ware; c. semi-vitreous table and toilet ware, ca. 1900, ware; d. porcelain decorative ware, ca. 1890–ca. 1905, ware.

FIGURE 212. Sebring Pottery Company: a. ironstone tableware, ca. 1895, ware; b. ironstone ware, ca. 1905, Modern Stamp; c. ironstone table and toilet ware, ca. 1895, ware; d. ironstone table and toilet ware, ca. 1895, ware.

UNCLE WIGGILY
REG. U. S. PAT. OFF.
COPYRIGHT 1924 BY
FRED A. WISH, INC.
NEW YORK CITY
SEBRING POTTERY CO.,
SOLE MANUFGRS.

a

b

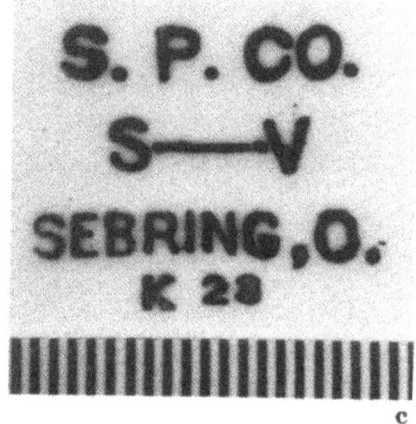

S. P. CO.
S——V
SEBRING, O.
K 28

c

d

FIGURE 213. Sebring Pottery Company: a. semi-vitreous baby plates, ca. 1925 (1924), ware; b. hotel china, 1900–ca. 1925, Modern Stamp; c. semi-vitreous tableware, ca. 1925 (1928), ware; d. semi-vitreous tableware, ca. 1925–ca. 1940 (1925), ware.

FIGURE 214. Sebring Pottery Company: a. semi-vitreous ware, ca. 1920–ca. 1940, ware; b. semi-vitreous ware, 1921–1943, ware; c. semi-vitreous ware, ca. 1920–ca. 1935, ware.

FIGURE 215. Sebring Pottery Company: a. semi-vitreous tableware, ca. 1925–ca. 1936 (1925), ware, also "New Era"; b. semi-vitreous tableware, ca. 1925–ca. 1942, Quality Stamp, see variations and pattern names in Figure 215c, d; c. semi-vitreous tableware, ca. 1925–ca. 1942, Quality Stamp, variations include: "Astoria," "Buddha," "Corinthian," "Green Wheat," "Golden Ware," "Metropolitan," "The Aristocrat," "The Jubilee," "Pegasus," "Rose Bower," variation of Figures 215b, d; 218a–d; d. semi-vitreous tableware, ca. 1925–ca. 1942, Quality Stamp, variation of Figures 215b, c; 218a–d.

FIGURE 216. Sebring Pottery Company: a. semi-vitreous tableware, ca. 1928, ware; b. semi-vitreous tableware, ca. 1928, ware; c. semi-vitreous tableware, ca. 1940, ware; d. semi-vitreous tableware, ca. 1930–1948, ware.

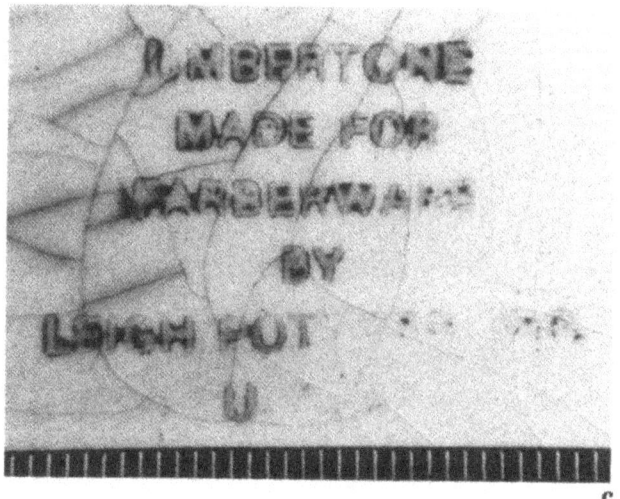

FIGURE 217. Sebring Pottery Company/Crescent China/Leigh Pottery: a. semi-vitreous ware, ca. 1925–ca. 1943, Quality Stamp; b. semi-vitreous tableware, ca. 1925–ca. 1940, ware; c. semi-vitreous tableware, 1926–1932, ware.

FIGURE 218. Sebring Pottery Company (Leigh Pottery Company): a. semi-vitreous tableware, 1926–1932, ware; b. semi-vitreous tableware, 1926–1932, Quality Stamp, variation of Figures 218a, c, d; 215b, c, d; c. semi-vitreous tableware, 1926–1932, ware, variation of Figures 218a, b, d; 215b, c, d; d. semi-vitreous cooking ware, 1926–1932, ware, variation of Figures 218a, b, c; 215b, c, d.

E. H. SEBRING CHINA COMPANY (Figure 219)   ca. 1908–1929

The E. H. Sebring China Company developed from the Oliver China Company around 1908 when Ellsworth Sebring purchased the pottery from his brother George. This firm produced semi-vitreous dinnerware, tea sets, and assortments of ware used for premiums. In 1929 the E. H. Sebring China Company joined the American Chinaware Corporation which was to declare bankruptcy in 1931 (McKee 1966: 40, 41; China and Glass Trade Directory 1927: 33–52; Mss. ELMC American Chinaware Corporation, Records of Formation 1929, American Chinaware Corporation, Bankruptcy Claim #23656 1931; Youngstown Daily Vindicator 2 February 1937).

a

c

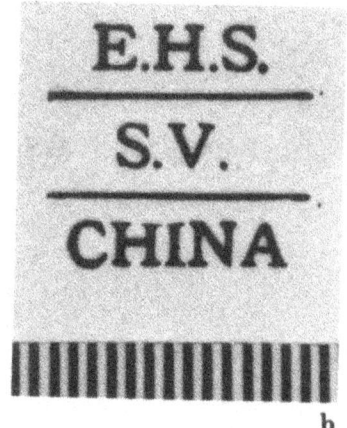

b

d

FIGURE 219. E. H. Sebring Pottery Company: a. semi-vitreous tableware, 1908–1929, ware: b. semi-vitreous tableware, 1908–1929, company advertisement; c. semi-vitreous tableware, 1908–1929, ware; d. semi-vitreous ware, ca. 1925, Quality Stamp.

SEVRES CHINA COMPANY (Figure 220)   1900–1908
WARNER-KEFFER CHINA COMPANY (Figure 221)   1908–1911

In 1900 Harry Keffer, Frank Crook, William Tebutt, Walter B. Hill, and William H. Deidrick purchased the former Sebring Pottery and began operations as the Sevres China Company. The firm produced semi-porcelain dinner, toilet, and tea sets. The corporation did not prosper and Tebutt, Hill, and Crook dropped out after only a few years. In 1908 J. R. Warner, formerly of the National China Company, entered the organization and its name was changed to the Warner-Keffer China Company. Difficulties arose and the pottery declined; it finally closed in 1911 (Mss. ELMC, Company stationery 1902; Illustrated Glass and Pottery World 1900: 8; USPA 1911: 15).

FIGURE 220. Sevres China Company: a. semi-vitreous table and toilet ware, 1900–1908, ware, also "Belmar"; b. semi-vitreous table and toilet ware, 1900–1908, Barber (1904: 117), variation of Figure 220a, also "Geneva," "Melton"; c. hotel china, 1900–1908, Barber (1904: 117).

FIGURE 221. Warner-Keffer China Company: a. semi-vitreous table and toilet ware, 1908–1911, ware; b. semi-vitreous table and toilet ware, 1980–1911, ware, decal; c. semi-vitreous table and toilet ware, 1908–1911, ware; d. semi-vitreous table and toilet ware, 1908–1911, Modern Stamp.

SMITH-PHILLIPS CHINA COMPANY (Figures 222–226)   1901–1929

In May 1901 Josiah T. Smith, William H. Phillips, Will S. Smith, Wilson F. Smith, and W. H. Griggs formed a corporation for the manufacture of pottery and china. The Smith-Phillips China Company operated the former "Klondyke" pottery of the Sebrings, which had been built in 1895. The new corporation produced a single line of semi-porcelain dinnerware named "American Girl," two toilet ware shapes—"Fenix" and "Kosmo," semi-porcelain hotel ware, and a variety of specialty items including cake plates, jugs, nuts bowls and spittoons. By the mid-1920s, the firm had dropped toilet wares and added more lines of dinnerware. Despite several changes in management, the plant operated steadily under its original name until 1929 when the corporation voted to join the American Chinaware Corporation. When that conglomerate folded after two years, Smith-Phillips ceased operations (Mss. ELMC, Company ledger 1901–1917, Company catalog ca. 1905; McCord 1905: 173; China and Glass Trade Directory 1927: 26, Mss. ELMC, American Chinaware Corporation ledger 1929).

FIGURE 222. Smith-Phillips China Company: a. semi-vitreous toilet ware, 1902–ca. 1920, ware; b. semi-vitreous toilet ware, ca. 1902–ca. 1920, Barber (1904: 106); c. semi-vitreous dinnerware, ca. 1904–ca. 1920, Barber (1904: 106); d. semi-vitreous hotel ware, ca. 1910 company catalog.

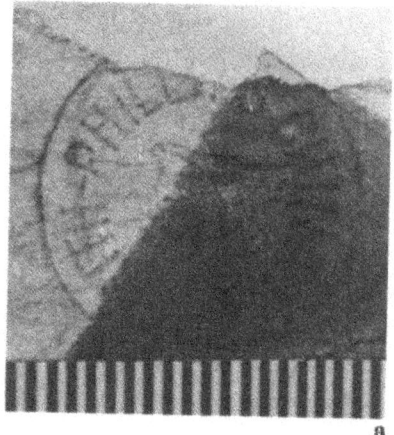

FIGURE 223. Smith-Phillips China Company: a. semi-vitreous ware, 1901–ca. 1915, Modern Stamp, mark reads: "Smith-Phillips China" with a pitcher in center; b. semi-vitreous tableware, 1906-4/1907, ware; c. semi-vitreous tableware, 1901–1929, ware, variation of Figure 223d; 224a–d; 226a; d. semi-vitreous tableware, 1901–1929, ware, variation of figure 223c; figure 224a–d; 226a.

FIGURE 224. Smith-Phillips China Company: a. semi-vitreous tableware, 1903, company ledger, note ticks at bottom—date is indicated by number and placement of ticks; b. semi-vitreous tableware, 1904, ware, variation of figure 223c–d; 224a, c, d; 226a; c. semi-vitreous tableware, 1905, ware, variation of figure 223c–d; 224a, b, d; 226a; d. semi-vitreous tableware, 1906-4/1907, ware, variation of figure 223c–d; 224a, b, c; 226a.

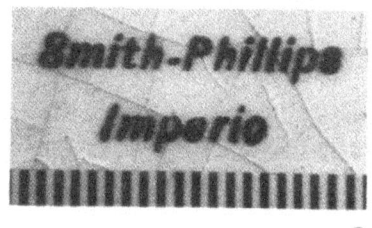

FIGURE 225. Smith-Phillips China Company: a. semi-vitreous tableware, 1909–ca. 1920, ware, also "St. Regis," "Fenix," "Cable," "Hotel"; b. semi-vitreous tableware, ca. 1915, ware, also "Alamo," "Alondra," "Buena Vista," "Carvel," "Orador," "Randolph"; c. semi-vitreous tableware, ca. 1915, ware, variation of Figure 225b; d. semi-vitreous tableware, ca. 1918, Modern Stamp, also "Martha Washington."

FIGURE 226. Smith-Phillips China Company: a. semi-vitreous tableware, 1901–1929 (1920), ware, variation of figures 223c, d; 224a, b, c, d.

FIGURE 226 continued. b. semi-vitreous tableware, ca. 1918–1929, ware; c. semi-vitreous tableware, ca. 1918–1929, ware, line name variation of figure 226b; d. semi-vitreous tableware, ca. 1918–1929 (1925) ware.

THE STANDARD POTTERY COMPANY (Figures 227–228)   1886–1927

The Standard Pottery Company began operations as a co-operative venture in 1886 with A. C. Gould as President. The pottery workers issued $30,000 in capital stock and began producing plain ironstone and decorated toilet and dinnerwares. The following year (1887) three kilns were in operation and the firm employed an average of 55 operatives, many of whom were also stockholders. The company characterized their operation as a ". . . co-operation of labor and capital and the highest efficiency of mechanical appliances and skilled labor" (Business Review 1887: 25).

The Standard Pottery Company, ignoring the wage reductions imposed by other East Liverpool firms in 1894, was one of the only local potteries to operate throughout the ensuing six-month strike. Soon after the strike, however, the co-operative plan was abandoned and the company re-organized under the leadership of Patrick McNicol (Calhoun 1922: 115–17; McKee 1966: 25).

The Company expanded its product lines and its physical plant during the next few years. By 1915 it produced semi-porcelain hotel, dinner, and toilet wares. In 1898 the firm built a six kiln plant in Salem, Ohio, and in 1904 it acquired the former Burford pottery in East Liverpool. This expansion, however, was short-lived and the firm sold both of these plants in 1920. In the meantime the Cronin family assumed control of the company with Daniel Cronin as president. The Standard Pottery Company continued to operate until 1927 when Cronin moved to New Cumberland, West Virginia, and organized the Cronin China Company (Mss. ELMC, Company catalog 1915; Calhoun 1922: 115–17; USPA 1904: 61; China and Glass Trade Directory 1927: 26; Obituary of Daniel Cronin, USPA 1939: 4).

FIGURE 227. The Standard Pottery Company: a. ironstone ware, 1886–ca. 1910, Modern Stamp, see similar mark Figure 13c, d; b. ironstone sanitary ware, 1886–ca. 1910, ware; c. ironstone hotel ware, 1886–ca. 1910, Modern Stamp.

FIGURE 228. The Standard Pottery Company: a. semi-vitreous dinnerware, ca. 1910–circa 1925, Modern Stamp; b. semi-vitreous dinnerware, ca. 1910–1927, ware; c. semi-vitreous dinner and serving ware, ca. 1915–1927 (1925), ware.

STERLING CHINA COMPANY (Figures 230–244)   1917–PRESENT

In 1917 a group of men which included Charles Pomeroy, A. B. Allen, and William Wells occupied the former Patterson Brothers pottery in Wellsville, Ohio, and founded the Sterling China company. The group refitted the yellow ware plant and began producing vitreous hotel china. Pomeroy was elected president of the company in 1923, a position he retained until his death in 1943, at which time his son William succeeded him. During the late 1930s and early 1940s, the firm completed several additions to its pottery and expanded its product lines. By 1949 the Sterling China Company was one of the three largest producers of vitrified hotel and restaurant china in the world. During World War II, Sterling supplied the bulk of the dinnerware used by the United States Armed Forces (Obituary of Charles C. Pomeroy, USPA 1943; The Wellsville Press 28 October 1949: 1; Calhoun 1922: 152; Mss. ELMC Company catalog, n.d.).

Although the Sterling China Company produced a wide variety of decorations on its hotel ware, for the most part its wares conform to traditional styling and design. The one major exception was a line designed by Russel Wright which the firm produced from the end of World War II until 1950. Produced in four colors (ivy green, straw yellow, suede gray, cedar brown), this streamlined table ware represented a bold departure from customary shapes and colors (Mss. ELMC, Company brochure ca. 1952; William Pomeroy 1981, pers. comm.).

The Sterling China Company continued to expand during the mid-20th century. In 1954 Sterling absorbed the Scammell China Company, a Trenton, New Jersey, competitor, and produces the former company's line of Lamberton China to the present day. Beginning in 1951, the firm also began operating a plant in Puerto Rico where it produced a line of ware known as "Caribe China." This plant was closed in December 1976. From Sterling's inception in 1917, until the present time, the company has given its location as East Liverpool in its literature, advertising, and pottery marks. Its plant, however, has always been located in nearby Wellsville (William Pomeroy 1981, per. comm.; McKee 1966: 33).

FIGURE 229. The Sterling China Company: a. semi-vitreous ware, 1936–1954, company stamp.

b

c

d

FIGURE 229 continued. b. semi-vitreous ware, ca. 1940, Quality Stamp; c. vitreous ware, ca. 1950–ca. 1960, company stamp; d. semi-vitreous ware, 1935–ca. 1950, ware.

FIGURE 230. The Sterling China Company: a. semi-vitreous ware, ca. 1940–ca. 1950, company stamp; b. semi-vitreous hotel ware, ca. 1940–ca. 1950, ware; c. semi-vitreous ware, ca. 1945–ca. 1960, company stamp; d. semi-vitreous ware, ca. 1945–ca. 1955, company stamp.

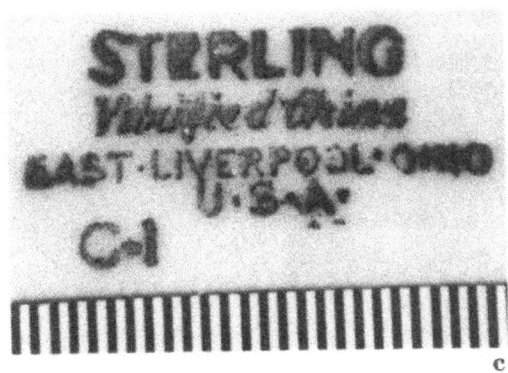

FIGURE 231. Sterling China Company: a. vitreous hotel and restaurant ware, ca. 1946–1954, ware; b. vitreous hotel ware, ca. 1946–present, ware, mark in color; c. vitreous hotel ware, ca. 1946–present, ware; d. vitreous dinnerware, ca. 1945–ca. 1955, ware.

FIGURE 232. Sterling China Company: a. vitreous dinnerware, ca. 1946–ca. 1959, company stamp; b. vitreous hotel dinnerware, ca. 1946–ca. 1959, ware, mark in color.

FIGURE 232 continued. c. vitreous hotel dinnerware, ca. 1949, Quality Stamp; d. vitreous hotel dinnerware, ca. 1949, ware, impressed.

FIGURE 233. Sterling China Company: a. vitreous institutional ware, ca. 1950–1966, company stamp; b. vitreous institutional ware, 1955–present, company stamp; c. vitreous institutional ware, ca. 1960, ware; d. vitreous institutional ware, ca. 1964, ware.

FIGURE 234. Sterling China Company: a. vitreous institutional ware, 1954–present, ware; b. vitreous institutional ware, ca. 1970, ware, (decal); c. vitreous institutional ware, ca. 1950, ware; d. vitreous institutional ware, ca. 1950, ware.

FIGURE 235. Sterling China Company: a. vitreous institutional ware, ca. 1950–ca. 1960, company stamp; b. vitreous institutional ware, ca. 1970–present, company stamp; c. vitreous institutional ware, ca. 1970–present, company stamp; d. vitreous institutional ware, ca. 1972–present, company stamp.

FIGURE 236. Sterling China Company: a. vitreous kitchen ware, ca. 1945–ca. 1965, ware; b. vitreous kitchen ware, ca. 1945–ca. 1965, company stamp; c. vitreous kitchen ware, ca. 1945–ca. 1965, company stamp.

FIGURE 237. Sterling China Company: a. vitreous serving ware, ca. 1968, ware; b. vitreous serving ware, ca. 1968, company stamp; c. vitreous serving ware, ca. 1972, company stamp, see similar mark figure 61a; d. vitreous serving ware, ca. 1972, company stamp.

FIGURE 238. Sterling China Company: a. vitreous serving ware, ca. 1960, company stamp; b. vitreous serving ware, ca. 1975, company stamp; c. vitreous dinner and serving ware, ca. 1965, company stamp; d. vitreous institutional ware, ca. 1960, company stamp.

FIGURE 239. Sterling China Company: a. vitreous institutional ware, ca. 1960, company stamp; b. vitreous institutional ware, ca. 1950–ca. 1960, company stamp; c. vitreous institutional ware, ca. 1970–present, ware; d. vitreous dinnerware, ca. 1965, ware.

FIGURE 240. Sterling China Company: a. vitreous institutional ware, ca. 1950–ca. 1960, company stamp; b. vitreous institutional ware, ca. 1950–1970, company stamp; c. vitreous hotel ware, ca. 1965, company stamp.

FIGURE 241. Sterling China Company (Caribe): a. vitreous institutional ware, ca. 1951–1976, company stamp; b. vitreous institutional ware, 1951–1976, company stamp; c. vitreous institutional ware, 1951–1976, company stamp.

FIGURE 242. Sterling China Company (Caribe): a. vitreous institutional ware, 1951–1976, company stamp; b. vitreous institutional ware, 1951–1976, Quality stamp; c. vitreous institutional ware, 1951–1976, company stamp; d. vitreous institutional ware, 1951–1976, company stamp.

FIGURE 243. Sterling China Company (Caribe): a. vitreous institutional ware, 1951–1976, company stamp; b. vitreous institutional ware, 1951–1976, company stamp; c. vitreous institutional ware, 1951–1976, company stamp; d. vitreous institutional ware, 1951–1976, company stamp, size variation of Figure 243c.

FIGURE 244. Sterling China Company (Caribe): a. vitreous institutional ware, ca. 1951–1976, ware; b. vitreous institutional ware, ca. 1951–1976, company stamp; c. vitreous institutional ware, 1951–1976, company stamp.

TAYLOR, LEE AND SMITH (Figure 245a)   1899–1901
TAYLOR, SMITH AND TAYLOR (Figures 245–264)   1901–1972/(1981)

John H. Taylor (of Knowles, Taylor and Knowles) and Charles A. Smith originally organized a company in 1899 to produce plain and decorated semi-porcelain. Soon after the initial organization, Joseph Lee and two of Taylor's sons, Homer J. and William L., joined the firm, which became known as Taylor, Lee and Smith. John Taylor intended to start his sons in the pottery business with this new venture. The company built an eight kiln pottery in Chester, West Virginia, which is directly across the Ohio River from East Liverpool. By the fall of 1900, Taylor, Lee and Smith began production in the new plant. When Lee withdrew from the firm in September 1901, the name was changed to Taylor, Smith and Taylor. Following several years of unsatisfactory operations, Smith briefly closed the plant. The firm was reorganized in 1906 when William L. Smith and his son acquired the Taylor interests. They resumed operations at the plant and retained the name of Taylor, Smith and Taylor. The pottery produced semi-vitreous dinner and toilet wares as well as products for hotels and restaurants. During the late 1930s, Taylor, Smith and Taylor introduced "Lu-Ray" and "Vistosa," both solid color dinnerwares, which became two of its most popular lines. In December of 1972, it was announced that the plant was to be sold to the Anchor Hocking Corporation.

The plant is currently operated by Anchor Hocking's ceramic products division as a subsidiary. However, on 28 September, 1981, officials of the Anchor Hocking Corporation announced that because of the "very depressed" dinnerware market they would close the Chester plant as of 31 December 1981 (The Evening News Review 11 January 1900, 10 September 1900, 26 October 1901; Calhoun 1922: 173, 138; China and Glass Trade Directory 1927: 33–52; Mss. ELMC, Company catalogs n.d.; East Liverpool Review 22 December 1922, 28 September 1981, 29 September 1981).

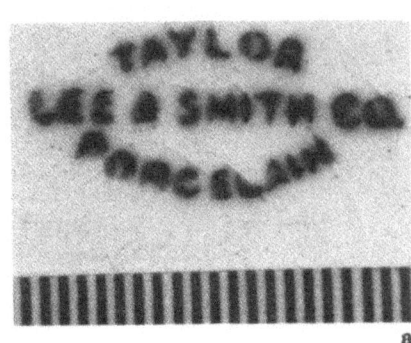

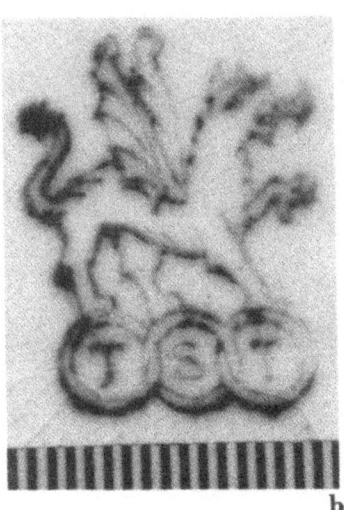

FIGURE 245. Taylor, Lee and Smith/Taylor, Smith and Taylor: a. semi-vitreous ware, 1900–1901, ware, also "Granite"; b. semi-vitreous ware, 1901–ca. 1930, ware, also: "Vitreous."

FIGURE 245 continued. c. semi-vitreous ware, 1901–ca. 1930, ware, variation of Figure 245b; d. hotel ware, ca. 1908–ca. 1930, ware.

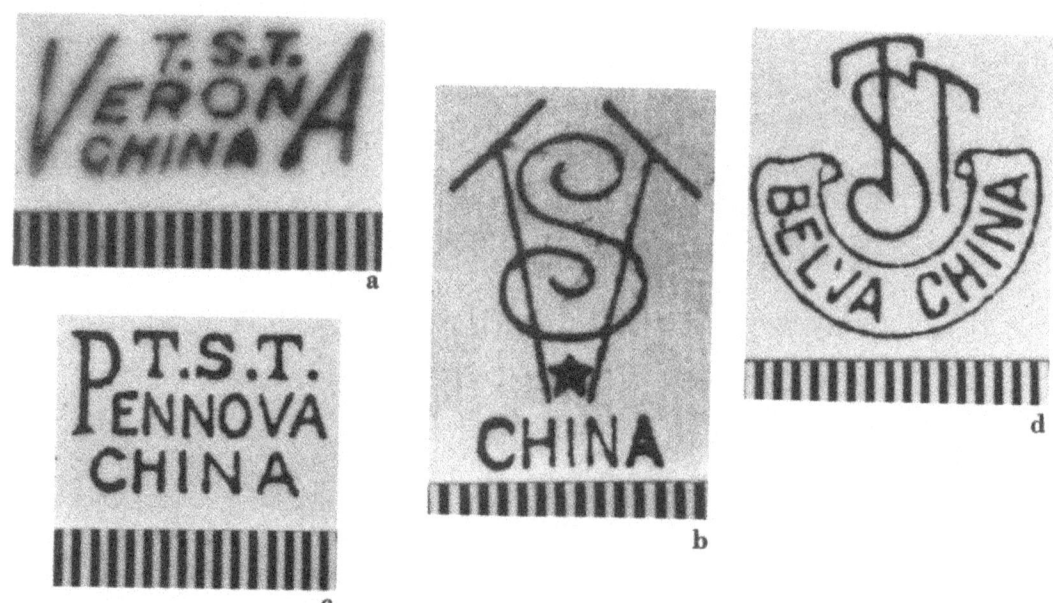

FIGURE 246. Taylor, Smith and Taylor: a. semi-vitreous ware, ca. 1915, ware; b. semi-vitreous ware, 1908–ca. 1915, ware; c. semi-vitreous ware, ca. 1920, company records; d. semi-vitreous ware, ca. 1920, Quality Stamp.

FIGURE 247. Taylor, Smith and Taylor: a. semi-vitreous tableware, ca. 1925 (1924), ware; b. semi-vitreous tableware, 1917–ca. 1925, ware; c. semi-vitreous tableware, ca. 1930 (1933), ware; d. semi-vitreous tableware, ca. 1935, ware.

FIGURE 248. Taylor, Smith and Taylor: a. semi-vitreous tableware, ca. 1935, ware; b. semi-vitreous tableware, 1928–ca. 1945 (1929), ware; c. semi-vitreous tableware, ca. 1938–ca. 1945, ware; d. semi-vitreous tableware, ca. 1940–ca. 1955, ware.

FIGURE 249. Taylor, Smith and Taylor: a. semi-vitreous dinnerware, 1939–ca. 1950, ware; b. semi-vitreous tableware, 1945–ca. 1953 (1950), ware, also "Cockerel," "Day Lily," "Magnolia," "Oakleaf"; c. semi-vitreous tableware, 1945–ca. 1955, variation of figure 249b; d. semi-vitreous tableware, 1954–1957 (1955), company stamp.

FIGURE 250. Taylor, Smith and Taylor: a. semi-vitreous tableware, ca. 1963–ca. 1968, ware; b. semi-vitreous table-ware, ca. 1965, ware, patterns include: "American Splendor," "Autumn Splendor" 1960, "Dianthus" 1960, "Echo Dell," "Happy Talk," "Ivory Tower," "Masterpiece," "Pretty Pink," "Rasberry," "Rhapsody," "Rose Sachet" 1960, "Rose Sunset," "Silver Wheat," "Wild Rice"; c. semi-vitreous tableware, ca. 1965, company information; d. vitreous table-ware, 1956–ca. 1962, ware.

FIGURE 251. Taylor, Smith and Taylor: a. semi-vitreous tableware, 1953–ca. 1960, company stamp, also: "Granite," "Sunburst," "Teal"; b. semi-vitreous tableware, 1953–ca. 1960 (1957), ware; c. semi-vitreous tableware, ca. 1955, ware, Quaker Oats premium; d. semi-vitreous tableware, ca. 1960, ware.

FIGURE 252. Taylor, Smith and Taylor: a. semi-vitreous tableware, ca. 1935–ca. 1960 (1951), ware also without "U.S.A."; b. semi-vitreous tableware, ca. 1930–ca. 1950, Quality Stamp; c. semi-vitreous tableware, ca. 1960, ware.

FIGURE 253. Taylor, Smith and Taylor: a. semi-vitreous tableware, ca. 1963, company stamp; b. semi-vitreous tableware, ca. 1963, company stamp, variation of figure 253a, also "Windemer," "Woodhue"; c. semi-vitreous tableware, ca. 1965, company stamp; d. semi-vitreous tableware, ca. 1968, company stamp.

FIGURE 254. Taylor, Smith and Taylor: a. ironstone-type tableware, ca. 1960, ware; b. cooking ware, ca. 1960, ware, impressed; c. cooking ware, ca. 1965, ware, mark reads: "Genuine/Oven Serve/Ware/T.S. & T./U.S.A"; d. semi-vitreous tableware, ca. 1965, company stamp, also "Autumn Bouquet," "Checks and Daiseys," "Old Plymouth," "Raspberry."

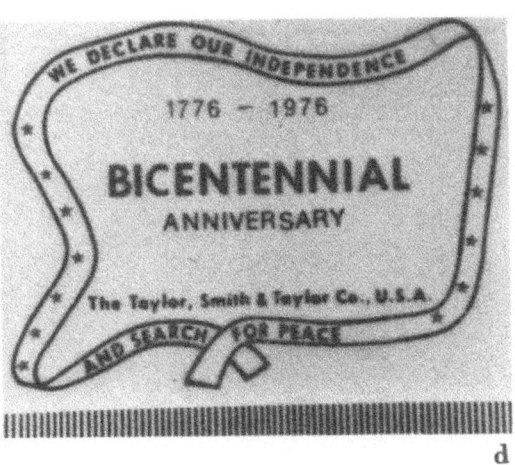

FIGURE 255. Taylor, Smith and Taylor: a. ironstone-type tableware, 1967–ca. 1975, color stamp; b. ironstone-type tableware, 1967–ca. 1975, company stamp; c. ironstone tableware, 1970, company stamp, also "Lancaster," "Lazy Daisy"; d. semi-vitreous ware, 1976, ware, decal.

FIGURE 256. Taylor, Smith and Taylor: a. ironstone-type tableware, ca. 1968, Quality Stamp; b. ironstone-type table-ware, ca. 1968, Quality Stamp, variation of Figure 256a, c, d; c. ironstone-type tableware, ca. 1965, company stamp, variation of Figure 256a, b, d; d. ironstone-type tableware, ca. 1968, company stamp, variation of Figure 256a, b, c.

FIGURE 257. Taylor, Smith and Taylor: a. ironstone-type tableware, ca. 1970, Quality Stamp; b. ironstone-type tableware, ca. 1972, company stamp, variation of Figure 257a, patterns include: "Aztec," "Champagne," "Flower Tree," "Gingham Garden," "Indian Morn," "Lilac Wreath," "Love Song," "Mountain Meadow," "Morning Glory," "Pette Bouquet," "Pink Posie," "Plaid," "Sierra," "Springdale," "Springtime," "Yellow Gingham," "Williamsburg Wheat," "Wood Rose"; c. ironstone-type tableware, ca. 1970, ware, also "Blue Moon"; d. ironstone-type tableware, ca. 1970, ware, also "Golden Oak."

FIGURE 258. Taylor, Smith and Taylor: a. oven ware, ca. 1957, company stamp; b. oven ware, ca. 1957, company stamp, size variation of Figure 258a; c. oven ware, ca. 1957, company stamp, variation of Figure 258a, b, d; d. oven ware, ca. 1957, company stamp, variation of Figure 258a, b, c.

FIGURE 259. Taylor, Smith and Taylor: a. semi-vitreous tableware, ca. 1960, company stamp, also: "Bleuclaire"; b. semi-vitreous tableware, ca. 1960, company stamp, see mark 134d; c. semi-vitreous tableware, ca. 1960, Quality Stamp.

FIGURE 260. Taylor, Smith and Taylor: a. oven ware, ca. 1958, company stamp; b. semi-vitreous ware, 1953–ca. 1957, company stamp; c. oven ware, ca. 1958, company stamp.

FIGURE 261. Taylor, Smith and Taylor: a. ironstone-type tableware, ca. 1965, ware, "Classic" is a shape name; b. ironstone-type tableware, ca. 1960, company stamp, shape name; c. ironstone-type tableware, ca. 1960, company stamp, shape name; d. ironstone-type tableware, ca. 1968, ware, shape name.

FIGURE 262. Taylor, Smith and Taylor: a. ironstone-type tableware, ca. 1972, Quality Stamp; b. ironstone-type tableware, ca. 1972, Quality Stamp; c. kitchen ware, ca. 1960, company stamp; d. semi-vitreous ware, ca. 1965, company stamp.

FIGURE 263. Taylor, Smith and Taylor: a. ironstone-type ware, ca. 1955, company stamp; b. ironstone-type ware, ca. 1970, company stamp; c. ironstone-type tableware, ca. 1965, company stamp; d. ironstone-type ware, ca. 1965, company stamp.

FIGURE 264. Taylor, Smith and Taylor: a. ironstone-type ware, ca. 1957–ca. 1968, company stamp; b. ironstone-type ware, ca. 1965, company stamp; c. semi-vitreous tableware, ca. 1970, company stamp; d. serving ware, 1957–ca. 1962, ware.

THOMAS CHINA COMPANY (Figure 265a, b)   1900–1905
(R. THOMAS AND SONS 1873–1957) (Figure 265c)

As a producer of semi-porcelain dinnerware, the Thomas China Company was short-lived. However, the parent company, R. Thomas and Sons, was a major force in the American ceramic industry for more than 60 years. The R. Thomas and Sons Company began operations in East Liverpool during the summer of 1873 when it drew its first kiln of door and furniture knobs, and their "American Knob Works" operated steadily during its early years (Thomas diary 1846–1878).

The development of the telephone and the incandescent light bulb during the late 1870s and early 1880s required a good insulation medium; vitrified ceramics proved to be the ideal substance. R. Thomas and Sons produced the first electrical insulators in January 1885. By 1892, when the firm was incorporated, the Thomases had discontinued the manufacture of knobs and devoted the entire plant to the production of low and high voltage insulators. The corporation's 1894 catalog offered nearly 300 types of insulators (Company History 1923; Calhoun 1922: 146).

In 1900 Richard Thomas' sons began construction of a six-kiln plant in Lisbon, Ohio, and by 1902 began production of semi-porcelain dinnerware. The huge demand for electrical porcelain, however, dictated the conversion of this plant to the production of insulators in 1905. Both plants prospered and in 1927 the firm sold its East Liverpool plant and moved the entire operation to its Lisbon location. R. Thomas and Sons discontinued business in 1957 (Calhoun 1922: 146; Vodrey 1945: 288).

Author's note: Although marks from electrical porcelain are not included in this study, it was deemed necessary to include information about R. Thomas and Sons because of the direct relationship between the two firms. One R. Thomas and Sons mark occurring on blue vases, (not on electrical procelain) which were probably company premiums, is included.

FIGURE 265. Thomas China Company/R. Thomas and Sons, Co.: a. semi-vitreous tableware, 1902–1905, ware; b. semi-vitreous tableware, 1902–1905, ware; c. vitreous vases, ca. 1900, ware, company premium.

C.C. THOMPSON POTTERY COMPANY (Figures 266–272)   1868–1938

The C.C. Thompson Pottery Company originated in 1868 under the name of Thompson and Herbert. Cassius C. Thompson, the son of a well-to-do dry goods merchant, and J. T. Herbert, a former crockery salesman, formed a partnership and built a small pottery near the Ohio River for the production of "Rockingham and Yellow Queensware." Two years later, in 1870, Josiah Thompson, Cassius' father, and his partner Basil Simms, acquired Herbert's interest in the business. The firm became known as C.C. Thompson and Company (Mss. ELMC, Company business card 1868; Barber 1893, reprint ed. 1976: 208).

Under this new management the firm prospered. By 1881 it employed 200 workers and anticipated enlargements which would double its output to $150,000 annually. This expansion was realized in September 1883 when the firm drew its first kiln of c.c. ware from its new four kiln plant. C.C. Thompson and Company offered bowls, nappies, plates, pitchers, teapots, mugs, sugars, covered dishes, bedpans, spittoons, and toilet sets in its c.c. line. With the exception of its toilet sets, the company also produced the same items in Rockingham and yellow ware (Columbiana County Directory 1881: 859; ELT 8 September 1883; Mss. ELMC, Company catalog, ca. 1886).

Following the death of Josiah Thompson in 1889, the firm incorporated as the C.C. Thompson Pottery Company. At about the same time, it added white ironstone toilet and dinnerwares to its expanding line. By 1917 the Thompsons had phased out yellow ware, Rockingham, and c.c. ware, and had begun to manufacture semi-porcelain dinnerware. On 19 September 1938, George C. Thompson, president of the firm, announced that because of poor business conditions and ". . . unsatisfactory sales prices. . . ." the business would cease operations (McCord 1905: 678, 705; Barber 1893, reprint ed. 1976: 208; Vodrey 1945: 284; East Liverpool Review 19 September 1938).

FIGURE 266. C. C. Thompson Pottery Company: a. c.c. tableware, 1883–1890, ware; b. ironstone tableware, 1890–ca. 1910, ware.

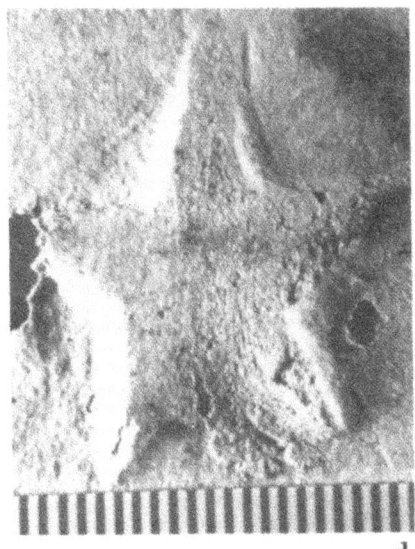

FIGURE 266 continued. c. c.c. or ironstone tableware, ca. 1894, ware; d. c.c. tableware, ca. 1890–ca. 1915, ware, raised.

FIGURE 267. C. C. Thompson Pottery Company: a. ironstone toilet ware, 1890–ca. 1908 Barber (1904: 110); b. ironstone toilet ware, 1890–ca. 1908 Barber (1904: 110); c. ironstone toilet ware, 1890–ca. 1908 Barber (1904: 110); d. ironstone tableware, 1890–ca. 1908 Barber (1904: 110).

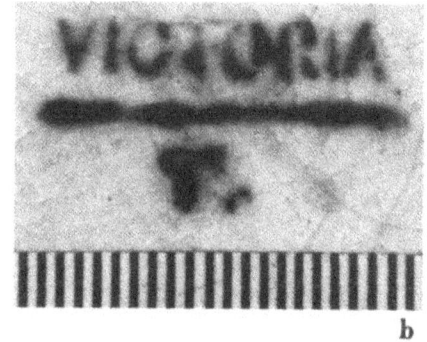

FIGURE 268. C. C. Thompson Pottery Company: a. yellow ware tableware, ca. 1905, ware, paper label; b. ironstone tableware, ca. 1925, ware; c. semi-vitreous tableware, ca. 1920, ware; d. semi-vitreous tableware, ca. 1920, ware.

FIGURE 269. C. C. Thompson Pottery Company: a. ironstone ware, ca. 1915, Modern Stamp; b. ironstone ware, ca. 1915, ware; c. ironstone ware, ca. 1915, Modern Stamp; d. semi-vitreous tableware, ca. 1920–ca. 1930, ware.

FIGURE 270. C. C. Thompson Pottery Company: a. ironstone kitchen and sanitary ware, ca. 1915, ware; b. ironstone kitchen and sanitary ware, ca. 1915, ware, variation of Figure 270s; c. semi-vitreous tableware, ca. 1920–ca, 1935, ware; d. semi-vitreous tableware, ca. 1920–ca. 1935, ware, impressed variation of Figure 270c.

a

c

d

b

FIGURE 271. C. C. Thompson Pottery Company: a. semi-vitreous tableware, ca. 1927–1938, ware, also: "Aladdin," "Seville"; b. semi-vitreous kitchenware, ca. 1933, ware; c. semi-vitreous kitchenware, ca. 1932–1938, ware, also: "Iris," "Mayfair"; d. semi-vitreous kitchenware, ca. 1932–1938, ware.

FIGURE 272. C. C. Thompson Pottery Company: a. semi-vitreous tableware, ca. 1916–1938, ware; b. semi-vitreous tableware, ca. 1916–1938, ware, also: "Francis," "Glenwood," "Heirloom Jade," "Oregon," "Princess," "Sydney"; c. semi-vitreous dinnerware, ca. 1933–1938, ware.

TRENLE CHINA COMPANY (Figures 273–274a, b) 1909–ca. 1942
TRENLE BLAKE CHINA COMPANY (Figure 274c, d) ca. 1942–1966

In 1909 Gus Trenle changed the name of the East End China Company to the Trenle China Company. The firm maintained the East End China lines of ware until 1917. At that time it converted its production to vitreous hotel and restaurant ware and electrical porcelain. In 1937 the Trenle China Company moved to Ravenswood, West Virginia. By 1942 the firm's name had been changed to the Trenle-Blake China Company with H. W. Blake as president. Trenle-Blake ceased operations in 1966 (USPA 1909: 13; Vodrey 1945: 286; China and Glass Red Book, 1942: 48; W. T. Blake 1981, pers. comm.).

FIGURE 273. Trenle China Company: a. semi-vitreous table and toilet ware, 1909–1917, ware; b. semi-vitreous table ware, 1909–1917, ware, variation of figure 273a, c, "Virginia" is a line name, see East End China Company, figure 29b; c. semi-vitreous tableware, 1909–1917, ware, variation of figure 273a, b, see East End China Company, figure 29b; d. semi-vitreous ware, 1909–1917, Modern Stamp.

FIGURE 274. Trenle China Company/Trenle-Blake China Company: a. vitrified hotel china, 1917–1937, ware; b. vitrified hotel china, 1917–1937, ware, variation of Figure 274d; c. vitrified hotel china, ca. 1940–1966, ware; d. vitrified hotel china, ca. 1940–1966, ware, variation of Figure 274b.

UNION CO-OPERATIVE POTTERY COMPANY (Figure 275–276)   1894–1900
UNION POTTERIES COMPANY   1900–1905

The Union Co-operative Pottery Company was organized by a group of East Liverpool operatives during a six-month strike in 1894. The workers pooled their resources and purchased the idle Wyllie pottery. F. G. Croxall became president of the newly formed company and by 1895 the company produced ironstone china and railroad sanitary ware. In November 1900 the company was placed in receivership and it was announced that the pottery would close as soon as all the orders were filled. However, it appears that only the co-operative feature of the firm was dropped because the pottery continued to function as the Union Potteries Company until 1905 (China, Glass and Lamps August 1894; Mss. ELMC, Company stationery 1895; Illustrated Glass and Pottery World November 1900; McCord 1905: 160).

FIGURE 275. Union Co-operative Pottery Company: a. ironstone dinnerware, 1894–1905, ware; b. ironstone tableware, 1894–1905, ware.

FIGURE 276. Union Co-operative Pottery Company: a. ironstone ware, 1894–1905, ware; b. ironstone toiletware, 1894–1905, ware; c. ironstone toilet and dinnerware, 1898–1905, ware.

UNITED STATES POTTERY COMPANY (Figure 277)   1898–1932

In 1898 Robert Hall, Sr., Silas M. Ferguson, and John J. Purinton formed a partnership and began construction of a new six kiln plant in Wellsville, Ohio. The United States Pottery Company produced semi-porcelain toilet and dinner wares. Following a fire at the pottery in 1900, the firm joined five other potteries to form the East Liverpool Potteries Company (see history) in 1901. When that organization finally disbanded in 1907 after six years of problems, the United States Pottery returned to its former individual status. Based on extant evidence, it appears that this firm continued to operate under the title of East Liverpool Potteries company even though it was a single firm. In 1932 the company suspended operations (Calhoun 1922: 154; Illustrated Glass and Pottery World October 1900; China and Glass Trade Directory 1927: 16; USPA 1933: 7). There is no evidence that a United States Pottery Company existed in East Liverpool as Barber states (1904, reprint ed. 1976: 113).

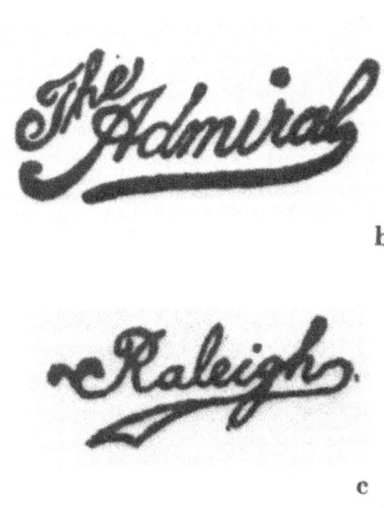

FIGURE 277. United States Pottery Company: a. semi-vitreous tableware, 1899–1901/1907–ca. 1920, ware; b. semi-vitreous toiletware, 1899–1901, ware, shape name; c. semi-vitreous ware, 1899–1901, Barber (1904: 113); d. semi-vitreous ware, 1899–1901, Barber (1904: 113).

VODREY ASSOCIATIONS (Figures 278–283)   1847–1928

Jabez Vodrey and his family first arrived in East Liverpool in 1847. A native of Staffordshire, England, Jabez worked at potteries in Pittsburgh, Pennsylvania; Louisville, Kentucky and Troy, Indiana prior to his landing in the small Ohio River town of East Liverpool. For a brief time after settling in East Liverpool, Vodrey manufactured clay smoking pipes. By 1848 he had formed a partnership with William Woodward, a prosperous local farmer, to produce yellow ware and Rockingham. Their small pottery was destroyed by fire in March of 1848 but Vodrey and Woodward, bolstered by financial support from two new partners, James and John S. Blakeley, began to rebuild the pottery. The Blakeley brothers operated a dry goods store and warehouse in East Liverpool.

The new firm of Woodward, Blakeley and Company erected a new brick pottery, appropriately named the ''Phoenix'' pottery, and began to manufacture yellow ware, Rockingham, and a line of terra cotta products. By 1852 the growing company consisted of five buildings, three large kilns, and employed from 70 to 80 workers. During that same year the firm won a gold medal for its ware from the American Institute (Thomas, John diary 28 March 1847; Vodrey, Jabez diary 12 January 1833, 29 March 1839, 22 July 1847, 10 March 1849; American Patriot 20 June 1848, 13 March 1849, 24 February 1852).

During the mid-1850s, Woodward, Blakeley and Company experienced many difficulties. Internal disputes, flood damage, a strike, and poor business conditions resulting from a recession destroyed the partnership. By the end of 1857, Vodrey's three sons, William, James, and John, were busy converting a nearby abandoned Catholic Church into a pottery. They also purchased adjoining land from Josiah Thompson in order to expand their operations. By the spring of 1858, the Vodrey and Brother Pottery Company was producing Rockingham and yellow ware. In that year, Woodward, Blakely and Company discontinued business. The ''Phoenix Pottery'' was sold at a sheriff's sale in 1859 (Vodrey, Jabez diary 1852–1858; WP 19 January 1858; Mss. ELMC Article of Agreement 11 December 1857; Pioneer 1876).

During its first years of operation, the Vodrey Pottery, known as the ''Palissy Works,'' felt the impact of unfavorable economic conditions and the disruptive effects of the Civil War. In addition, Jabez Vodrey died in 1861 and his son John was killed while fighting for the Union Army.

Following the war, the firm prospered. It continued to manufacture Rockingham and yellow wares until 1876 when the firm constructed new buildings and kilns and began the production of white ironstone. Although the Vodrey pottery never became one of the giants of the East Liverpool district, it prospered during its tenure. In 1896 the firm was incorporated as the Vodrey Pottery Company and semi-porcelain was added to its ironstone line. During the first quarter of the 20th century, the firm produced white granite and semi-porcelain dinner sets, toilet wares, and hotel china. The Vodrey Pottery Company suspended operations in 1928 (Mss. ELMC Vodrey and Brother price list 1865; Pioneer 1876; McCord 1905: 533; Mss. ELMC, Company price lists 1913, 1926, Vodrey 1945: 282).

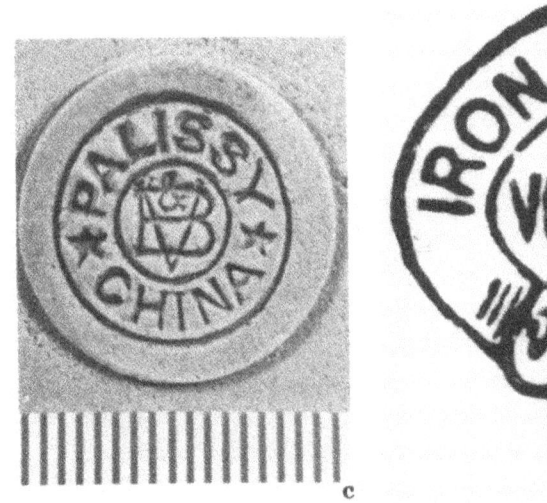

FIGURE 278. Vodrey and Brother Pottery Company: a. ironstone tableware, 1876–1896, ware; b. ironstone tableware, 1876–1896, brass stamp, mark on ware is stamped, not impressed; c. ironstone ware, 1876–1896, brass stamp, mark on ware is stamped, not impressed; d. ironstone tableware, 1876–1896, ware.

FIGURE 279. Vodrey and Brother Pottery Company: a. ironstone tableware, 1876–1896, ware; b. ironstone tableware, 1876–1896, ware, variation of figure 279a; c. ironstone tableware, 1876–1896, Barber (1904: 107), variation of figure 279a, b; d. ironstone toilet ware, 1876–1896, brass stamp, mark on ware is stamped, not impressed.

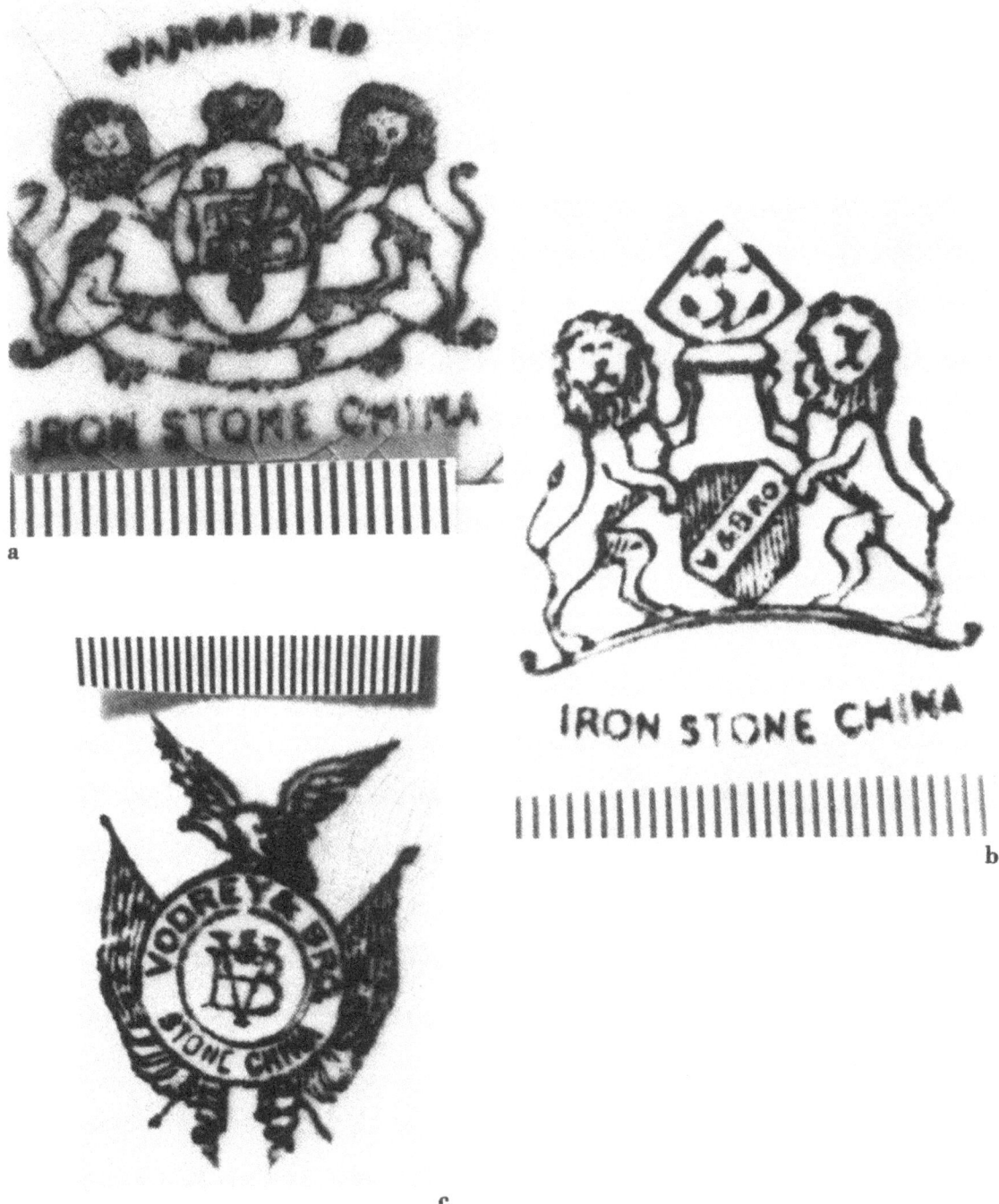

FIGURE 280. Vodrey and Brother Pottery Company: a. ironstone tableware, 1876–1896, ware; b. ironstone tableware, 1876–1896, ware; c. ironstone ware, 1876–1896, ware.

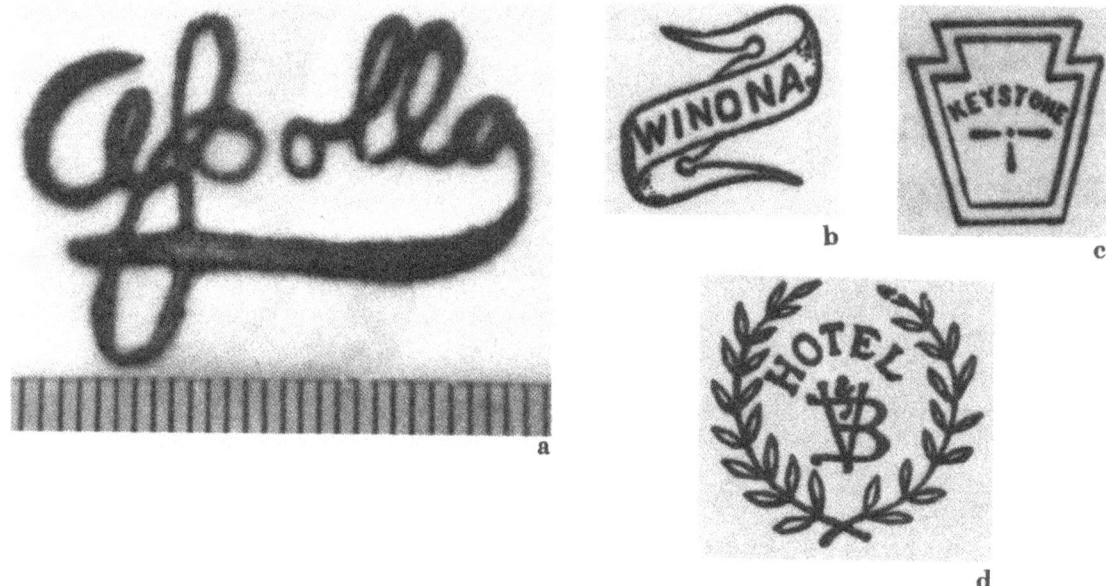

FIGURE 281. Vodrey and Brother Pottery Company: a. ironstone toilet ware, 1876–1896, ware; b. ironstone toilet ware, 1876–1896, Barber (1904: 107); c. ironstone hotel ware, 1876–1896, Barber (1904: 107); d. ironstone tableware, ca. 1900, Barber (1904: 107).

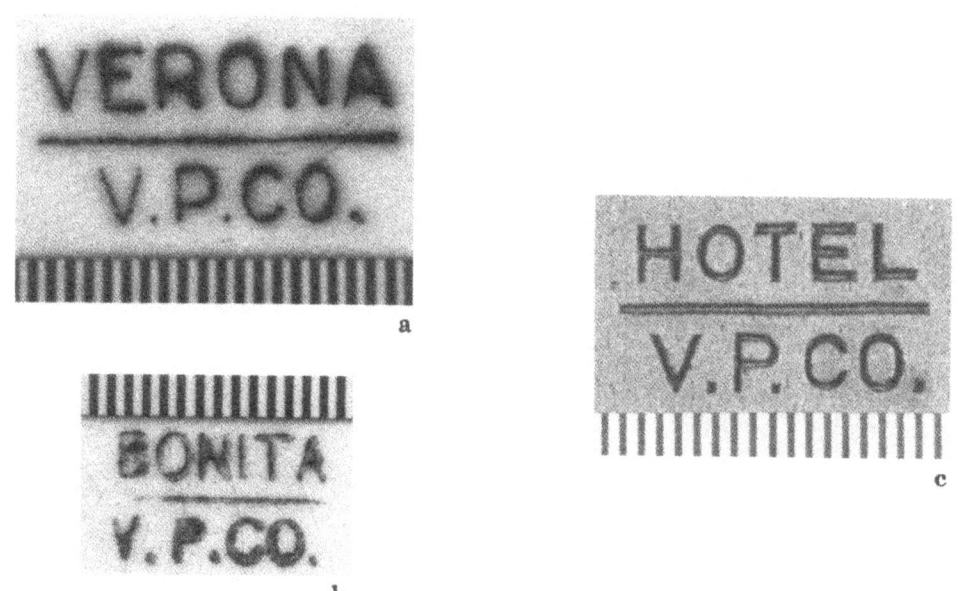

FIGURE 282. Vodrey Pottery Company: a. ironstone toilet ware, 1896–1928, ware, also "Admiral"; b. ironstone toilet ware, 1896–1928, ware; c. hotel ware, 1896–1928, brass stamp, mark on ware is stamped, not impressed.

FIGURE 283. Vodrey Pottery Company: a. semi-vitreous tableware, ca. 1910–1928, ware; b. semi-vitreous tableware, 1896–ca. 1920, ware, variation of Figure 283a; c. semi-vitreous tableware, ca. 1905–1929, ware; d. semi-vitreous hotel ware, ca. 1922, ware.

WALLACE AND CHETWYND (Figures 284–286)   1882–1901

The firm of Wallace and Chetwynd purchased the "Wedgewood" pottery from the Harker Pottery Company in 1881. The proprietors renamed the works the "Colonial" pottery and began producing white ironstone china on 4 March, 1882. Because the firm sacrificed quantity for quality, the "Colonial Pottery" was known for its excellent products. The firm continued to expand its toilet and dinner ware lines throughout the late 19th century. In 1884 the company announced that they had perfected an underglaze printing technique that would henceforth be used on all of its products (ELT 7 March 1882, 19 April 1884).

Wallace and Chetwynd merged with five other firms in 1901 to form the East Liverpool Potteries Company. When that organization faltered in 1903, the newly formed Colonial Company opened in the former Wallace and Chetwynd building (Genealogical and Family History of Eastern Ohio 1903: 468).

Extant pieces in the East Liverpool Museum of Ceramics range from plain white ironstone to highly decorated pieces of table and toilet wares. Although some pieces are hand painted and gilded, most were decorated with single color transfers in brown or green. The quality of Wallace and Chetwynd's decorations is excellent.

FIGURE 284. Wallace and Chetwynd: a. ironstone table and toilet ware, 1882–1901, ware, attributed; b. ironstone table and toilet ware, 1882–1901, ware; c. semi-vitreous table and toilet ware, ca. 1896, ware; d. ironstone table and toilet ware, 1882–1901, ware.

a

b

FIGURE 285. Wallace and Chetwynd: a. ironstone ware, 1882–1901, ware; b. ironstone ware, 1882–1901, ware, variation of Figure 285a.

FIGURE 285 continued. c. ironstone ware, 1882–1901, ware, impressed; d. ironstone ware, 1882–ca. 1890, ware.

FIGURE 286. Wallace and Chetwynd: a. ironstone ware, ca. 1890, ware; b. ironstone tableware, ca. 1896, ware.

WELLSVILLE CHINA COMPANY (Figures 287–293)   1902–1959 (1969)

In 1902 a company under the leadership of Monroe Patterson purchased the abandoned works of the former Pioneer Pottery Company in Wellsville, Ohio. The six kiln plant had been operated sporadically for the past 10 years under the previous owner. By 1912 the firm manufactured plain and decorated semi-porcelain dinner and toilet wares, tea sets, spittoons, sanitary items, accessory pieces, and assorted specialty items. Beginning in 1933, the Wellsville China Company added vitreous hotel porcelain to its production line. In March 1959, the Sterling China Company, also located in Wellsville, assumed controlling interest of the Wellsville China Company. Their intention was to provide technical and financial assistance so that the pottery could continue to operate as an independent division.

In December 1969, Sterling closed the pottery (Calhoun 1922: 151; Mss. ELMC, Company price list 1912; Vodrey 1945: 287; East Liverpool Review 4 March 1959; William Pomeroy 1981, pers. comm.).

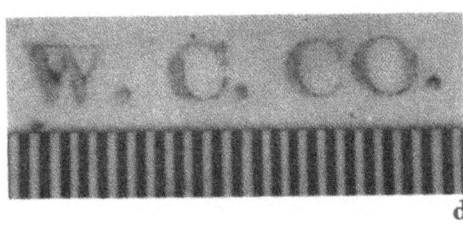

FIGURE 287. Wellsville China Company: a. semi-vitreous ware, 1902–ca. 1930, ware; b. semi-vitreous dinner and sanitary ware, ca. 1910–ca. 1930, ware; c. semi-vitreous table and toilet ware, ca. 1915–ca. 1925, ware; d. semi-vitreous ware, ca. 1920, ware.

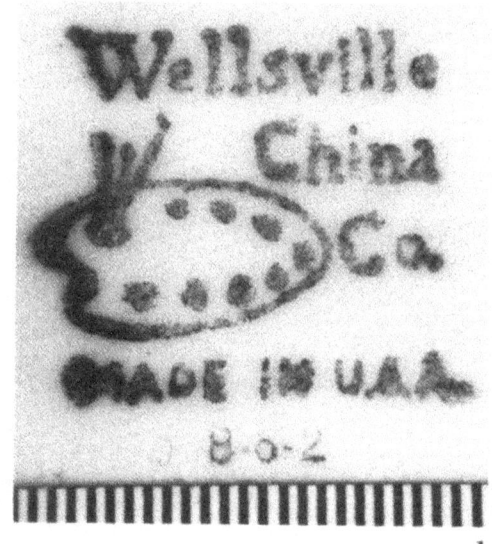

FIGURE 288. Wellsville China Company: a. semi-vitreous tableware, ca. 1935–ca. 1945; b. oven ware, ca. 1940–ca. 1950, Quality Stamp; c. semi-vitreous tableware, ca. 1940–ca. 1955, Quality Stamp; d. semi-vitreous tableware, ca. 1940–ca. 1960, ware.

FIGURE 289. Wellsville China Company: a. vitreous hotel ware, 1933–ca. 1960, ware; b. vitreous hotel ware, 1933–ca. 1960, ware; c. vitreous hotel ware, 1933–ca. 1960, ware, also: "Belmont," "Majestic"; d. vitreous hotel ware, ca. 1950, ware.

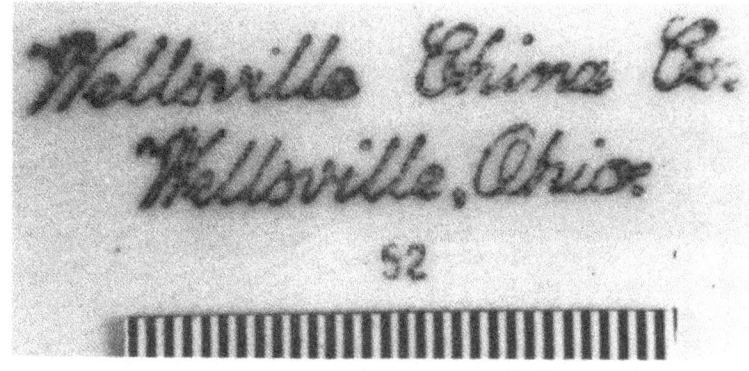

a

b

c

d

FIGURE 290. Wellsville China Company: a. vitreous hotel ware, ca. 1952, ware; b. vitreous hotel ware, ca. 1957, ware; c. vitreous hotel ware, ca. 1955, ware; d. vitreous hotel ware, 1933–ca. 1960, Quality Stamp.

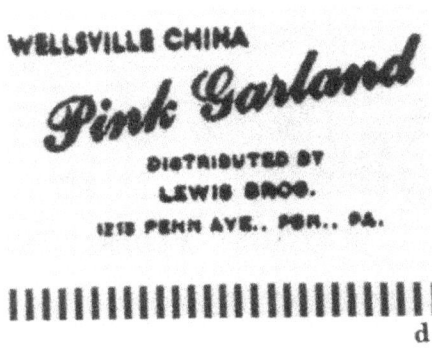

FIGURE 291. Wellsville China Company: a. vitreous hotel ware, ca. 1958, ware; b. vitreous hotel ware, ca. 1960, ware; c. vitreous hotel ware, ca. 1960, ware, variation of figure 291b; d. vitreous hotel ware, ca. 1960, Quality Stamp.

FIGURE 292. Wellsville China Company: a. vitreous hotel ware, ca. 1955, Quality Stamp; b. vitreous hotel ware, ca. 1955, Quality Stamp; c. vitreous hotel ware, ca. 1955, Quality Stamp; d. vitreous hotel ware, ca. 1955, Quality Stamp, size variation of figure 292c.

a

b

c

FIGURE 293. Wellsville China Company: a. vitreous hotel ware, ca. 1960, Quality Stamp; b. vitreous hotel ware, ca. 1960, Quality Stamp; c. tableware, ca. 1960, ware.

WEST END POTTERY COMPANY (Figure 294–296)   1893–1938

The West End Pottery Company began operations in 1893 following the reorganization of Burgess and Company. The latter firm, which operated the "American China Works," failed to find a market for their bone china and was forced to reorganize and produce semi-vitreous wares. The new firm was composed of seven individuals including William Burgess, John Peake, Willis Cunning, and George Ashbaugh. The potting skills of Peake and Cunning coupled with the sales experience of Ashbaugh and the business sense of Burgess, helped the company to expand. The West End Pottery Company manufactured semi-porcelain and white granite (ironstone) dinner, toilet, and hotel wares as well as specialty items (Calhoun 1922; 85–87; Mss. ELMC, Company order sheet, ca. 1895).

During the late 1890s, the company experienced many changes in ownership as partners traded stock or left the firm. Despite the changes, it continued to thrive and by 1925 it remained one of East Liverpool's most prosperous small potteries. By 1927 the company had stopped the production of ironstone and offered semi-vitreous dinnerware, hotel ware, tea sets, toilet ware, premium assortments, druggist's specialties, and hospital ware. The West End Pottery Company suspended operations in 1938 (Calhoun 1922: 88; China and Glass Trade Directory 1927: 33–52; Vodrey 1945: 286).

FIGURE 294. West End Pottery Company: a. ironstone toilet ware, 1893–ca. 1910, Modern Stamp; b. ironstone tableware, 1893–ca. 1910, ware; c. vitreous hotel ware, ca. 1915, Modern Stamp; d. semi-vitreous ware, ca. 1915, ware, other shapes: "Cable," "Columbia," "Duchess," in dinnerware; "Atlantic," "Cuban," "Pacific" in toiletware; "Hotel" in double-thick hotel ware.

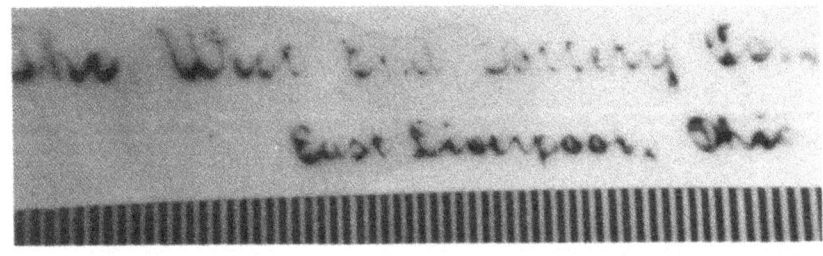

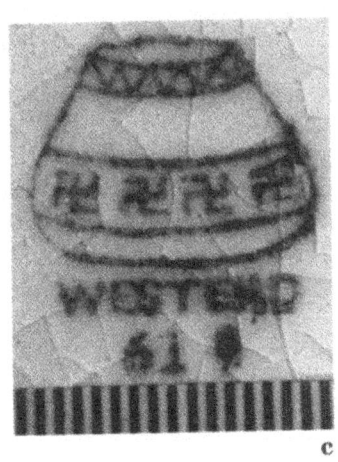

FIGURE 295. West End Pottery Company: a. ironstone sanitary ware, ca. 1916 (1914), Modern Stamp; b. semi-vitreous tableware, ca. 1926, ware, not a production mark; c. semi-vitreous tableware, ca. 1920–ca. 1932, ware; d. semi-vitreous ware, ca. 1933, company price list, attributed mark.

FIGURE 296. West End Pottery Company: a. semi-vitreous tableware, 1928–1938, ware; b. semi-vitreous tableware, 1928–1938, ware, variation of figure 296a, c; c. semi-vitreous tableware, 1928–1938, ware, variation of figure 196a, b.

JOHN WYLLIE AND SON (Figure 297)   1874–1893

John Wyllie, an English potter, worked in a variety of potteries on the European continent and in the United States prior to his arrival in East Liverpool. In 1874 Wyllie purchased the "Great Western Pottery Works" from the firm of William Brunt and Son who had manufactured Rockingham and yellow ware in the plant. Wyllie and his son, John Jr., refurbished and re-equipped the pottery for the production of white ironstone. This was the fifth whiteware pottery established in East Liverpool since 1872 (Annual Business Review of Columbiana County, Ohio 1887: 26; Liverpool Democrat, 2 October 1874).

By 1881 the firm had doubled its production capacity and employed more than 80 workers. John Wyllie, Sr. died the following year, but his son continued to operate, and even expand, the business. The Wyllie pottery specialized in sanitary goods and toilet ware for hotels, steamships, and railroads and produced large orders for the Pullman Company. In March 1884, the firm introduced ceramic stove hole plates with a variety of decorations including landscapes and floral motifs (Columbiana County Directory 1881; Annual Business Review of Columbiana County 1887: 26; ELT 21 March 1885; East Liverpool Review 1 March 1884).

The operation of the pottery continued on an intermittent basis until 1893 when John Wyllie, Jr. died. The Union Co-operative Pottery Company took over the abandoned plant in 1894 (Calhoun 1922: 111; McCord 1905: 160).

The pottery of John Wyllie and Son produced a high quality white ironstone. While they were far from the largest in East Liverpool, their quality product indicates that they were always one of the most prominent.

FIGURE 297. John Wyllie and Son: a. ironstone toilet and tableware, 1875–ca. 1885, ware, also used by Knowles, Taylor, and Knowles of East Liverpool 1874–circa 1878, see figure 97a, and William Young and Sons, Trenton, New Jersey 1870–1879, initials at bottom'' "WYS," Barber (1904: 44–45); b. ironstone toilet and tableware, 1875–ca. 1888, ware, American and English shields also used by the Mercer Pottery Company, Trenton, New Jersey; International Pottery Company, Trenton, New Jersey; New York City Pottery, New York, New York, Barber (1904: 57, 58, 78); c. ironstone table and toilet ware, 1875–ca. 1888, ware, size variation of figure 297b; d. ironstone toilet and tableware, 1875–1893, ware.

REFERENCES

Abbreviations used in references

ACS	Bulletin of the American Ceramic Society
ELCD	East Liverpool City Directory
ELT	East Liverpool Tribune
Mss. ELMC	Manuscript collection, East Liverpool Museum of Ceramics
USPA	Proceedings of the United States Potters' Association (1889–1941)
	Annual Report of the United States Potters' Association (1942–1966)
WP	Wellsville Patriot (previously the American Patriot)

AMERICAN PATRIOT (BECAME WELLSVILE PATRIOT)
1845–1864

ANNUAL BUSINESS REVIEW OF COLUMBIANA COUNTY, OHIO.
1887   M. W. Thompson and Company, Canton, Ohio.

ANNUAL REPORT OF THE UNITED SATES POTTERS' ASSOCIATION
1942–1966

ANNUAL REPORT, STATE OF OHIO, BUREAU OF LABOR STATISTICS.
1877, 1879, 1895

BARBER, EDWIN ATLEE
1893   The Pottery and Porcelain of the United States.; reprint ed. (1976). Feingold and Lewis, New York.

BARBER, EDWIN ATLEE
1904   Marks of American Potters.; reprint ed. (1976), Feingold and Lewis, New York.

BARTH, HAROLD B.
1926   History of Columbiana County, Volume 1. Historical Publishing Company, Topeka-Indianapolis.

BULLETIN OF THE AMERICAN CERAMIC SOCIETY.
1937   "William Bloor," 16(1): 23–31.

BULLETIN OF THE AMERICAN CERAMIC SOCIETY.
1945   History of the Hall China Company, East Liverpool, Ohio, 24(8): 280–81.

CALHOUN, W. A.
1922   Early Clay Industries of the Upper Ohio Valley. Ms. on file, East Liverpool Museum of Ceramics, East Liverpool, Ohio.

CARSON, EDWARD
1973   Homer Laughlin, 1873–1973, The First Hundred Years. Ms. on file, East Liverpool Museum of Ceramics, East Liverpool, Ohio.

CERAMIC INDUSTRY
1938   A Century of Progress, 1838–1938, 31(6): 35–39.

CERAMIC TRADE DIRECTORY
1933, 1947–1948   Ceramics Publishing Company, Inc., Newark, New Jersey.

CHINA AND GLASS RED BOOK
1942–1952   China, Glass and Lamps, Pittsburgh, Pennsylvania.

CHINA AND GLASS TRADE DIRECTORY
1927–1941   China, Glass and Lamps, Pittsburgh, Pennsylvania.

COLUMBIANA COUNTY DIRECTORY
1881

CROCKERY DEALERS' YEAR BOOK
1902   Press of Jekins & McCowan, New York.

CROCKERY GLASS AND LAMPS
29 August 1894; 22 January, 28 February, 18 November 1896; 29 January 1897; 1917

CROCKERY AND GLASS JOURNAL
10 December 1915; 20 December 1917; 19 December 1918

DAILY CRISIS
1891   29 September 1891

DUKE, HARVEY
1977   *Superior Quality Hall China: A Guide for Collectors*. An ELO Book, (privately published).

EAST LIVERPOOL CITY DIRECTORIES
1898, 1899, 1915, 1921, 1926, 1934, 1937, 1948, 1950, 1955, 1958, 1961, 1978   R. L. Polk and Company, Columbus, Ohio and Pittsburgh, Pennsylvania.

EAST LIVERPOOL GAZETTE
16 August 1873, 25 August 1874

EAST LIVERPOOL MERCURY
1861–1862

EAST LIVERPOOL NEWS
1935   29 March 1935, 19 May 1935

EAST LIVERPOOL REVIEW
26 January, 1 February 1937; 19 September 1938; 26 March, 6 September 1940; 4 March 1959; 5 September 1962; 1 February 1963; 22 December 1972; 28 September, 29 September 1981

EAST LIVERPOOL TELEPHONE DIRECTORY
1952, 1968

EAST LIVERPOOL TRIBUNE
4 March 1876; 6 October 1877; 7 March 1882; January 1883; December 1884; 21 March 1885

EVENING NEWS REVIEW
29 October 1881; 1 March 1884; 11 January 1900; 26 September 1903; 16 January 1907

FINANCE AND INDUSTRY
1923   Clay Products Industry Enjoys Prosperity, 21 April: 7, 34.

GARRETT, BRICE
1966   Ohio's Lotus Ware. *Spinning Wheel: The National Magazine of Antiques* 22(1–2): 16–17.

GENEALOGICAL AND FAMILY HISTORY OF EASTERN OHIO
1903   Lewis Publishing Company.

GLASS AND POTTERY WORLD
1907, 1909

HOWE, HENRY
1899   *Historical Collections of Ohio*. Henry Howe and Son, Columbus.

ILLUSTRATED GLASS AND POTTERY WORLD
1896; October, November 1897; March, May 1898; May, November 1900.

KOVEL, RALPH M. AND TERRY H.
1953   *Dictionary of Marks: Pottery and Porcelain*. Crown Publishers, Inc., New York.

LEHNER, LOIS
1978   *Ohio Pottery and Glass: Marks and Manufacturers*. Wallace-Homestead Book Company, Des Moines, Iowa.

LEHNER, LOIS
1980   *Complete Book of American Kitchen and Dinner Wares*. Wallace-Homestead Book Company, Des Moines, Iowa.

LIVERPOOL DEMOCRAT
2 October 1874

MACK, HORACE
   1879   *History of Columbiana County.* D. W. Ensign and Company, Philadelphia.

MANUSCRIPT COLLECTION OF THE EAST LIVERPOOL HISTORICAL SOCIETY HOUSED AT THE OHIO HISTORICAL SOCIETY'S EAST LIVERPOOL MUSEUM OF CERAMICS
          (contains ledgers, catalogs, price lists, legal documents, photographs, manuscripts, trade publications, and other such resources which apply to the local pottery industry).

McCORD, WILLIAM B.
   1905   *History of Columbiana County.* Biographical Publishing Company, Chicago.

McKEE, FLOYD W.
   1966   The Second Oldest Profession: A Century of American Dinnerware Manufacture. (privately printed).

PIONEER POTTING SERIES
   1876   Typescript copy of series published in the East Liverpool Tribune, 18 March–24 June 1876.

PITTSBURGH MORNING POST
   13 November 1850

PITTSBURGH SUNDAY SUN-TELEGRAPH
   17 April 1938

POTTER'S GAZETTE
   21 June 1877

PROCEEDINGS OF THE UNITED STATES POTTER'S ASSOCIATION
   1889–1941

RAMSAY, JOHN
   1939   *American Potters and Pottery.* The Colonial Press, Inc., Clinton, Massachusetts.

R. THOMAS AND SONS COMPANY
   1923   Our 50th Year, (privately printed).

SEARS, ROEBUCK AND COMPANY CATALOG
   1902   Sears, Roebuck and Company, Chicago.

SPARGO, JOHN
1926   *Early American Pottery and China.* Century Company, New York.

SMITH, WILLIAM G.
   1888   *Early Reminiscences of "Fawcettstown" or East Liverpool.* (privately printed).

STEFANO, FRANK JR.
   1976   Ohio Pottery . . . Bennett and Vodrey, Potters at East Liverpool, Ohio. *Tri-State Trader* 8(49): 24–25.

STOUT, WILBUR
   1923   History of the Clay Industry in Ohio. In *Report of the Geological Survey of Ohio.* 4th series, Bulletin 26: 7-102. Geological Survey of Ohio, Columbus, Ohio.

THOMAS, JOHN DIARY
   2 July 1845–8 April 1878 (unpublished manuscript).

THORN, JORDON C.
   1947   *Handbook of Old Pottery and Porcelain Marks.* Tudor Publishing Company, New York.

UNITED STATES POPULATION CENSUS
   1840–1920   Miscellaneous reports and compendiums.

THE POTTERY INDUSTRY
   1915   U.S. Department of Commerce, miscellaneous series No. 21, U.S. Government Printing Office, Washington, D.C.

VODREY, JABEZ DIARY
   12 January 1833–22 June 1860   (unpublished manuscript).

VODREY, WILLIAM H.
   1945   Record of the Pottery Industry in East Liverpool District. *Bulletin of the American Ceramic Society*, August
          1945, pp. 282–288 (first published in Ohio Geological Survey Bulletin, 1923, pp. 74–81).

WADE, RICHARD C.
   1972   *The Urban Frontier: Pioneer Life in Early Pittsburgh, Cincinnati, Lexington, Louisville, and St. Louis*. The
          University of Chicago Press, Chicago and London (First published by Harvard University Press under the title
          The Urban Frontier: The Rise of Western Cities, 1790–1830).

WELLSVILLE PATRIOT (PREVIOUSLY THE *AMERICAN PATRIOT*)
   1845–1864

YOUNGSTOWN DAILY VINDICATOR
   2 January 1937

WILLIAM C. GATES, JR.
EAST LIVERPOOL MUSEUM OF CERAMICS
OHIO HISTORICAL SOCIETY
EAST LIVERPOOL, OHIO 43920

DANA E. ORMEROD
DEPARTMENT OF SOCIOLOGY/ANTHROPOLOGY
KENT STATE UNIVERSITY
EAST LIVERPOOL CAMPUS
EAST LIVERPOOL, OHIO 43920

Appendix A

Decorators and Distributors

A. C. BLAIR STUDIOS (Figure 298)   1945–1960

In 1945, A. C. Blair left his position at the Harker Pottery Company and started a decorator's business in Chester, West Virginia. Like the majority of small decorators, little information is available concerning Blair's operations or the reasons for his discontinuing business in 1960 (ELCD 1937: 440, 1961: 73).

FIGURE 298. A. C. Blair Studios: semi-vitreous decorated ware, 1945–1960, ware.

W. C. BUNTING COMPANY (Figures 299–300)   1947–PRESENT

Delmar T. O'Hara and Janet O'Hara started this business in the basement of their home in Wellsville, Ohio. Using the name of an established local merchant, W. C. Bunting (1880), and buying blanks from Acme, Hall, Scio, and other ceramic manufacturers, the O'Haras specialized in decorating personalized mugs for universities and fraternities.

Their first kiln had a one mug capacity, but as orders increased larger kilns were installed. The second kiln held 4 mugs, while the third held 30. In 1954 business growth dictated that they move out of their basement to a larger facility in Wellsville. One year later, further increases in orders made a second move necessary. The company resided at its third location until 1963 when they moved the business to its present East Liverpool address of 1425 Globe Street.

Del O'Hara remained as president of the company until his unofficial retirement in 1975. At that time, O'Hara's sons, Terry and Tim, assumed control of the company. Today, Bunting remains a leading decorating firm; they have expanded beyond the mug and stein market to include personalized specialty items such as glass tumblers and mixers, brown ceramic jugs, vases, ash trays, and plaques. Annual production over the past five years (1975–1980) has ranged from 600,000 to 700,000 pieces. (Terry and Tim O'Hara 1981, pers. comm.; Mss. ELMC, Company catalog n.d.).

FIGURE 299. W. C. Bunting Company: a. semi-vitreous specialty ware, 1947–1956, ware; b. semi-vitreous specialty ware, ca. 1955, ware; c. semi-vitreous specialty ware, 1955–1964, ware; d. semi-vitreous specialty ware, 1964–present, ware.

FIGURE 300. W. C. Bunting Company: a. vitreous and semi-vitreous specialty ware, ca. 1970–present, ware; b. vitreous and semi-vitreous specialty ware, ca. 1970–present, ware.

EAST LIVERPOOL ART CHINA COMPANY (Figure 301)   1898–ca. 1908

Started in 1898, the East Liverpool Art China Company was managed by Edward F. O'Connor. The company lists itself as manufacturers of Belleek ware and specialties. Pieces at the Museum of Ceramics are not Belleek, but are a pair of gaudy semi-vitreous vases. No evidence has been located to substantiate the claim that the company manufactured Belleek ware. By 1908, the East Liverpool Art China Company was no longer listed in city directories (ELCD 1898–1899: 114).

FIGURE 301. East Liverpool Art China Company: semi-vitreous specialties, 1898–ca. 1908 (1899), ware.

EAST LIVERPOOL CHINA COMPANY (Figure 302)   1947–PRESENT

The East Liverpool China Company was intended as the firm name for what became the W. C. Bunting Company. Unable to obtain financial backing for the unknown East Liverpool China Company, Delmar O'Hara utilized the established W. C. Bunting name. From the company's inception in 1947 O'Hara maintained the intended name and at present W. C. Bunting products are also marketed at retail under the East Liverpool China Company mark. (Mss. ELMC, Company catalog, n.d.; Terry and Tim O'Hara 1981, pers. comm.).

a

b

FIGURE 302. East Liverpool China Company: a. vitreous and semi-vitreous specialty ware, 1947–present, ware; b. vitreous and semi-vitreous specialty ware, 1947–present, company stamp.

MONARCH DINNERWARE COMPANY (Figure 303)   1937–1972 (PRESENT)

The Monarch Dinnerware Company was started in 1937 by Wilford Deven. Like many of the small decorators of the area, information concerning this company is limited. Monarch is listed as a wholesaler of china in 1941; by 1948 Deven is listed as operating The Gift Shop in Newell, West Virginia, apparently to distribute his decorated wares. In 1970, the W. C. Bunting Company purchased Monarch. Bunting moved the business to Wellsville and operated it as a separate company until 1972.

At that time, Bunting absorbed Monarch and now uses the Monarch name as a jobber in the distribution of its ware (ELCD 1937: 532, 1948: 529; Terry and Tim O'Hara 1981, pers. comm.).

FIGURE 303. Monarch Dinnerware Company: a. semi-vitreous decorated wares, 1937–1972, ware; b. semi-vitreous decorated ware, 1937–1972, company stamp.

OAKWOOD CHINA COMPANY (Figure 304)   1912 (1915)–ca. 1921

The earliest listing for the Oakwood China Company (not to be confused with East Liverpool Oakwood Pottery Company) is in the city directory of 1915 with James MacCamant as president. However, a piece in the Museum of Ceramics collection bears a 1912 date. This piece carries an Oakwood mark but it is not marked East Liverpool. Wares decorated by Oakwood are very distinctive. The Oakwood China Company purchased blanks from local and foreign firms and decorated them with a wood grain design which resembles a poor example of modern wood paneling. By 1921, both Oakwood and MacCamant had left the East Liverpool area. The authors have examined one piece of ware marked Oakwood of Ravenna, Ohio, which is identical to the decorated East Liverpool wares (ELCD 1915: 200, 390; 1921: 276).

FIGURE 304. Oakwood China Company: a. vitreous and semi-vitreous decorated ware, ca. 1915, ware; b. vitreous and semi-vitreous decorated ware, ca. 1915, ware; c. vitreous and semi-vitreous decorated ware, ca. 1915, ware; d. vitreous and semi-vitreous decorated ware, ca. 1915, ware.

THE PEARL CHINA AND POTTERY COMPANY (Figures 305–306)   1931–PRESENT

In 1931, George and Dennis Singer incorporated the Pearl China and Pottery Company as a pottery outlet. Prior to the incorporation, Dennis was an independent pottery salesman and George operated a grocery store in East Liverpool. In 1939, the Singers opened a new store at their present East Liverpool location and continued to distribute wares under the "Pearl China" mark. These wares were produced by the affiliated "Pioneer Pottery" (see history) and by the Homer Laughlin China Company. Pearl also served as an outlet for the other pottery companies still located in the East Liverpool district. (ELCD 1939: 286, 1926: 338, China, Glass & Lamps June 1939: 41–42). Today, Pearl China is an outlet for imported as well as domestic pottery and porcelain.

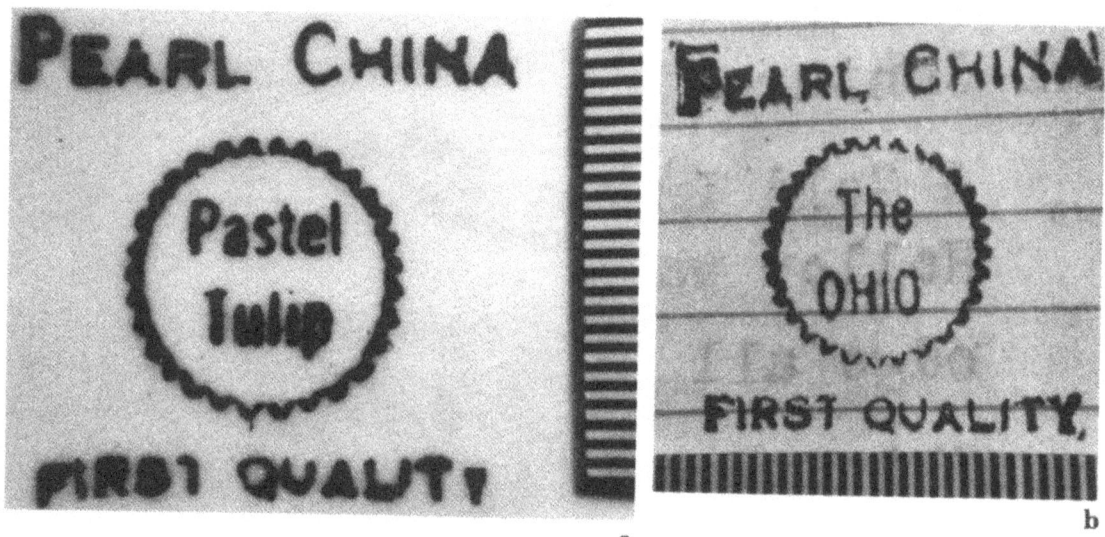

FIGURE 305. Pearl China and Pottery Company: a. vitreous and semi-vitreous decorated ware, 1931–1958, ware; b. vitreous and semi-vitreous decorated ware, 1931–1958, company stamp; c. vitreous and semi-vitreous decorated ware, 1931–1958, ware; d. vitreous and semi-vitreous decorated ware, 1931–1958, ware.

FIGURE 306. Pearl China and Pottery Company: a. vitreous and semi-vitreous decorated ware, 1931–1958, ware; b. vitreous and semi-vitreous decorated ware, 1931–1958, company stamp.

PINES POTTERY COMPANY (Figure 307)   1952–1967

Research has not revealed much information concerning the Pines Pottery Company. Founded in 1952, it is listed as being a wholesaler for ''Sayre China.'' Capitalizing on the East Liverpool name, Pines Pottery apparently utilized Sayre China as a ''house brand'' line of ware. In 1967, the business ceased operations (East Liverpool Phone Directory 1952: 74, 1968: 62).

FIGURE 307. Pines Pottery Company: a. vitreous and semi-vitreous decorated ware, 1952–1967, company stamp; b. vitreous and semi-vitreous decorated ware, 1952–1967, company stamp.

FIGURE 307 continued. c. vitreous and semi-vitreous decorated ware, 1952–1967, ware.

JOHN F. STEELE (Figure 308)   1878–1891

 Johnathan Steele came to East Liverpool from the Staffordshire district of England in 1878. A skilled decorator, Steele opened an independent shop soon after his arrival, and by 1881 he employed 10 people. He advertised that he would decorate ''china, table and toilet ware . . . with . . . monograms, crests, initials, and designs of every variety'' (Mss. ELMC Company stationery 188__; Columbiana County Directory 1881: 863).

 East Liverpool's 12 whiteware potteries would have kept Steele and other independent decorators very busy during the 1880s. By the 1890s, however, many local firms had instituted their own decorating departments and many of the independents either went to work for the potteries or left East Liverpool. Steele discontinued business in 1891. His mark may appear alone or in conjunction with a manufacturer's mark (Mack 1879: 183; Vodrey 1945: 287).

FIGURE 308. John F. Steele: ironstone decorated ware, 1878–1891, ware.

Appendix B

Double Stamps and Over Stamps

While researching this volume, wares were located which had been stamped with more than one mark. This could have been the result of carelessness on the part of an employee, however, it is more likely that these were instances of filling large orders from previously marked undecorated stock (Figure 309). On occasion, a manufacturer would receive an order too large to fill from either stock or rush production. Rather than refuse the order, the company would sub-contract with another pottery. This resulted in wares bearing the mark of two different manufacturers (Figure 310a). In addition, independent decorators also purchased blanks from a variety of manufacturers. Occurrence of both the decorator's and manufacturer's marks on a piece of ware not only aids in cross-dating the marks and ware, but also yields insight into the competitive markets of the era (Figure 310b, c.)

FIGURE 309. Appendix B, over stamps: a. Potter's Co-operative Company.

b

c

d

FIGURE 309 continued. b. Taylor, Smith and Taylor Company; c. Homer Laughlin China Company; d. Homer Laughlin China Company.

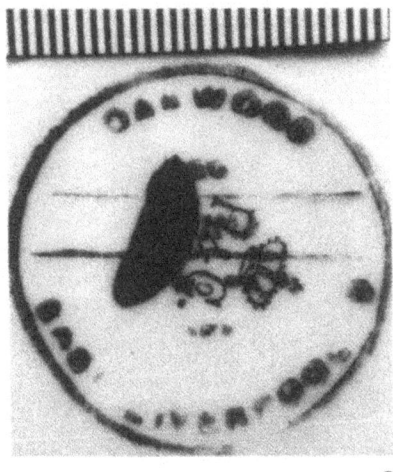

FIGURE 310. Appendix B, double stamps: a. Hall China Company and Taylor, Smith and Taylor; b. Oakwood China Company and Goodwin Pottery Company; c. Oakwood China Company and Unidentified European company.

Appendix C

Trade Marks Published as Back Stamps

Two readily available publications on American ceramics, *Ohio Pottery and Glass: Marks and Manufacturers* (Lehner 1978) and the *Complete Book of American Kitchen and Dinner Wares* (Lehner 1980), have erroneously identified several manufacturer's trade marks as back stamps. In order to avoid further confusion concerning the East Liverpool district manufacturers, these improperly listed marks are included. The trade marks listed in Figure 311 are cataloged in "Back Stamps and Trade Marks" (*Crockery and Glass Journal* 15 March 1954: 164–66).

The Homer Laughlin "gladiator" is used for advertisements (Figure 312a) and on containers for the packaging of ware (Figure 312b). These marks were never used on any production ware (Joseph Wells, Jr. and Ed Carson 1981 pers. comm.). Taylor, Smith and Taylor (T.S. & T.) also used specific trade marks other than on ware. Figure 313a was used as a letterhead and on shipping containers. John Gilkes, design director of T.S. & T. (presently Anchor Hocking Corporation), states that the detail of this trademark makes it impossible to replicate as a back stamp. Figure 313b was used in advertisements and never on ware (John Gilkes 1981, pers. comm.).

The Hall China Company letterhead is shown in Figure 314a. The full company name in conjunction with the zip code appears only on the company's stationery. The motif of Hall China's postage meter (Figure 314b) does not occur on any of their ware (Jack Hall and Everson Hall 1981, pers. comm.). Figure 314c was the trade mark used on Harker Pottery Company letterheads. The difference between Figure 314c and Figure 67b is the direction of the arrow through the bow and the placement of the company initials. No examples of ware with this mark (Figure 314c) have been located.

a

b

c

FIGURE 311. Appendix C: a. French Saxon China Company trademark, not a back stamp (Lehner 1980: 182); b. Homer Laughlin China Company trademark, not a back stamp (Lehner 1980: 187/upside down); c. Homer Laughlin China Company trademark, not a back stamp (Lehner 1978: 49, 1980: 187).

FIGURE 312. Appendix C: a. Homer Laughlin China Company, advertisement trademark, not a back stamp, (Lehner 1978: 49); b. Homer Laughlin China Company, packaging container trademark, not a backstamp (Lehner 1978: 49).

FIGURE 313. Appendix C: a. Taylor, Smith and Taylor Company, letterhead and shipping container trademark, not a back stamp, (Lehner 1978: 52, 1980: 195); b. Taylor, Smith and Taylor Company, advertisement trademark, not a back stamp, (Lehner 1980: 187).

a

b

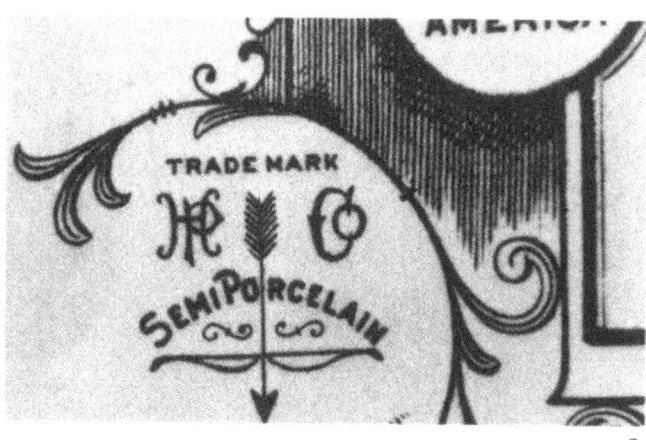

c

FIGURE 314. Appendix C: a. The Hall China Company, letterhead, full company name and zip code, (Lehner 1978: 46); b. The Hall China Company, postage meter tape, spurious mark, (Lehner 1978: 46, 1980: 185); c. The Harker Pottery Company, letterhead trademark, not a back stamp (Lehner 1980: 185, Kovel 1977: 160, Thorn 1947: 32, Ramsay 1939: 262, Spargo 1926: 366).

Appendix D

Other District Manufacturers and Decorators

The following is a list of known companies that either did not use marks to identify their products or whose marks have not been located or identified.

1.	Agner and Foutts	1863–1883
2.	Agner and Gaston	1883–1884
3.	American Porcelain Company	ca. 1922
4.	Artistic China Company*	undetermined at present
5.	Baggott Brothers	1853–ca. 1897
6.	Ball and Morris	1846–1856
7.	Barnhart Pottery Company*	ca. 1955
8.	James H. Baum (decorator)	1883–1884
9.	Belman Pottery Company	undetermined at present
10.	Belmonte China	ca. 1952
11.	Bel-Mar Pottery Company	ca. 1932
12.	Benty Brothers (Oakwood Art Pottery)	1900–1906
13.	Emanuel Booth	1876
14.	Burgess and Company	1890–1893
15.	Burgess, Webster and Viney	1867–1869
16.	William Burton	undetermined at present
17.	George Buxton	ca. 1885–1891
18.	Cameo China Company	ca. 1950
19.	Chic Pottery Company	1937–1945 (moved to Zanesville, OH)
20.	China and Vitreous Products Corporation	undetermined at present
21.	William Colclough	ca. 1850
22.	Craven Art Pottery	1905–ca. 1910
23.	Joseph Dennis	1875–1886
24.	Douds and Foutts	ca. 1872
25.	Dovey, Webster and Company	1848
26.	The Empire Company	ca. 1850
27.	Hermann Feustal*	ca. 1900
28.	Flentke, Harrison and Company	1877–ca. 1885
29.	Flentke, Worchester and Company	1874–1877
30.	Foster and Garner	ca. 1856–1859
31.	Foster and Rigby	ca. 1866–1868
32.	Foster and Rowley	1860–ca. 1866
33.	Fowler and O'Connor	1871–?
34.	Gamble and Surles	ca. 1878
35.	George Garner	ca. 1846
36.	Goodwin Pottery Company	1936–1940 (Different firm than Goodwin Pottery Co., 1844–1913)
37.	Thomas Haden	1874–1888
38.	Harker and Smith	1853–ca. 1856
39.	Harker, Thompson and Company*	1851–1854
40.	Henderson Pottery	ca. 1849–ca. 1854
41.	Hilton China Company	ca. 1915
42.	Horton Specialty Company	ca. 1936
43.	William Higginson	ca. 1897
44.	George F. Humrickhouse	1877–ca. 1883
45.	Jackson Brothers	1868–1870
46.	Jones Pottery	1867–1880
47.	Keramos Pottery Company*	ca. 1921

(Appendix D continued)

48. Knowles and Harvey	1854–ca. 1865
49. Larkins Brothers	ca. 1848–1861
50. Manton and Albright	ca. 1892
51. A. J. Marks and Company	1866–1869
52. Meric Art Studios (Subsidiary of the West End Pottery Company, ca. 1936–1938)	
53. William McCollough (Ramsay 1939: 217)	no further information available
54. McDevitt and Moore	1868–ca. 1900
55. McDonald Decorating Shop	ca. 1945
56. McGillvray and Orr	1855–1857
57. Newell, Larkins and Company	1848–ca. 1852
58. Edward O'Connor	ca. 1885
59. Purinton Pottery Company	1936–1942 (moved to Shippenville, PA)
60. Reston Art Ware Company	ca. 1930
61. T. Rigby and Company	1868–1872
62. Salt and Mear*	1842–ca. 1852/1856–ca. 1860
63. Scores China Company	ca. 1907
64. Simms and Starkey	1866–1868
65. N. M. Simms and Company	1868–1874
66. Sinclair Art Pottery	undetermined at present
67. Sprucevale Pottery	ca. 1852–1859
68. Starkey and Ourby	ca. 1870–1872
69. Trentvale Pottery	ca. 1900
70. United China Company	ca. 1921
71. Usona Art Pottery*	ca. 1932–ca. 1952
72. Wallace Brothers	1856–ca. 1861
73. Elijah Webster	1858–ca. 1861
74. Webster, Campbell and Company	1886–1888
75. Webster and Phillips	ca. 1848–1850
76. Joseph Wells	ca. 1826–ca. 1856
77. Wellsville Novelty Pottery Company	undetermined at present
78. West, Hardwick and Company	1867–1883
79. Woodward and Vodrey	1847–1849
80. Woodward, Blakeley and Company	1849–1857
81. Worchester, Bulger and Son	1872–1884
82. World Pottery and China Company	ca. 1921–ca. 1934

*Mark located too late for inclusion in this volume.

Appendix E

Guide to Manufacturers Names/Building Designations

In the past, numerous authors have confused the formal name of a manufacturer with the name applied by a firm to the actual pottery works or building. This confusion has led to the proliferation of inaccurate information and fallacies resulting in erroneous identifications of East Liverpool pottery producers and their marks. The following list provides the names of companies and the designations applied to individual buildings used in this text. Although other firms also occupied a particular pottery works, this list contains only those companies which incorporated that name into its identity.

Pottery works	Company name	Dates
American China Works	Burgess and Company	1890–1893
	West End Pottery Company	1893–1938
American Knob Works	R. Thomas and Sons Company	1873–1927
Broadway Pottery Works	T. Rigby & Company	1868–1872
	John Goodwin & Sons	1872–1875
	Goodwin Brothers Pottery Co.	1875–1893
	Goodwin Pottery Company	1893–1913
Buckeye Pottery Works	Flentke, Worcester & Co.	1874–1877
	Flentke, Harrison & Co.	1877–1881
	Knowles, Taylor & Knowles	1881–1929
Colonial Pottery	Wallace & Chetwynd	1882–1901
	The Colonial Co.	1903–1929
Diamond Pottery	Mountford & Co.	1891–1894
Dresden Pottery Works	Brunt, Bloor, Martin & Co.	1875–1882
	Potter's Cooperative Co.	1882–1925
	Dresden Pottery Co.	1925–1927
Eagle Pottery	John Goodwin	1844–1853
	Baggott Brothers	1853–ca. 1897
East Liverpool Porcelain Works	William Bloor	1860–1862
East Liverpool Pottery Works	Knowles & Harvey	1854–ca. 1865
	Isaac Knowles	ca. 1865–1870
	Knowles, Taylor & Knowles	1870–1929
Etruria Pottery	Harker, Taylor & Co.	1846–1851
	Harker, Thompson & Co.	1851–1854
	George S. Harker & Co.	1854–1890
	Harker Pottery Co.	1890–1931
Great Western Pottery Works	William Brunt Jr.	1867–1874
	John Wyllie & Son	1874–1893
Klondyke Pottery	French China Co.	1898–1901
	Smith-Phillips China Co.	1901–1929
Lincoln Pottery Works	West, Hardwick & Co.	1867–1883
	George Morley & Son	1884–1891
Mansion Pottery	Salt and Mear	1842–1853/ca. 1856–1865
	Harker and Smith	1853–ca. 1856
	Croxall and Cartwright	1863–1888
	J. W. Croxall & Sons	1888–1898
	Croxall Pottery Co.	1898–1914

(Appendix E continued)

Pottery works	Company name	Dates
Novelty Pottery Works	John Goodwin	1863–1866
	A. J. Marks & Co.	1866–1869
	McNicol, Burton & Co.	1869–1892
	D. E. McNicol Pottery Co.	1892–1928
Ohio Valley Pottery	Laughlin Brothers	1873–1877
	Homer Laughlin China Co.	1877–1929
Palissy Works	Vodrey & Brother	1858–1896
	Vodrey Pottery Co.	1896–1928
Phoenix Pottery	Woodward, Blakeley & Co.	1849–1857
	William Brunt Jr.	1859–1878
	William Brunt Son & Co.	1878–1892
	William Brunt Pottery Co.	1892–1911
Pioneer Pottery Works	Morley & Co.	1879–1884
	Pioneer Pottery Co.	1884–1900
Riverside Knob Works	William Brunt, Sr.	1850–1910
	General Porcelain Co.	1918–ca. 1938
Salamander Pottery Works	Morley, Godwin & Flentke	1857–1878
	Godwin & Flentke	1878–1882
	William Flentke	1882–1886
School House Pottery	Webster, Campbell & Co.	1886–1888
	James H. Baum	1888–1896
Union Pottery	Ball and Morris	1845–1856
	Croxall and Cartwright	1856–1888
	J. W. Croxall & Sons	1888–1898
	Croxall Pottery Co.	1898–1914
Wedgewood Pottery	Benjamin Harker & Sons	1877–1881

Appendix F
Index by Motif

In order to facilitate the identification of a particular mark, an index by motif has been created. This index is paramount if a mark is not easily assigned to a specific pottery or is not readily recognized as being from the East Liverpool district. The motifs have been divided into the various components or symbols that make up the mark and are categorized alphabetically according to those components. Marks involved in the alphabetic listings (block print and script) are arranged by either the first letter of a company's name or by the first letter of the most prominent word incorporated within the mark. Other entries include ware types, trade names, geometric shapes, animals, and other themes within the overall motif.

Oberlin—104d.

Ohio—9a, 10d, 21b, 25c, 27, 64a–b, 74b, 75a, 76a, 77c, 78, 80a, 107b, 109a, 114a, 149a, 150c, 151a–c, 152c–d, 153a–d, 156b, 158c, 159a–c, 161a–b, 165c, 166a, 176c, 188c, 199b–c, 200a, 200c, 201a–d, 202b, 204b, 205a–d, 206b, 208, 210b, 213c, 216a, 216d, 217a, 229d, 230a–c, 231b–c, 232a–b, 238d, 250c, 253d, 265c, 268a, 274a, 287b, 288a–b, 290a–b, 291a–c, 292b, 293a, 295b, 296a–c, 299a–d, 301, 302a, 305b–c, 306a, 307c.

Opaque China (printed)—284b–c, 286a.

Oval—21a, 53d, 54c, 62b, 68d, 86b, 87a–c, 88a, 88c–d, 90a, 92a–b, 95, 96, 128b, 157b, 169b, 181b, 186a–c, 191a–d, 207a, 211a, 227a–b, 253b, 254d, 255a–c, 299a, 307a–b.

Oven Proof (printed)—71b, 74d, 76c–d, 88b–d, 89b, 92a–b, 95, 124d, 138c–d, 140d, 141d, 145c, 207a–c, 250a–c, 251a–b, 253a–c, 254a, 254d, 255a–c, 256a–b, 256d, 257a–b, 258a–d, 260a, 260c, 261a–b, 261d, 262a–c, 263a–d, 264a–c, 271b.

Oven Serve (printed)—117a–c, 118a–d, 200d, 254b–c.

Oven Ware or Oven Tested (printed)—51a, 68c–d, 129a.

P (block print)—38d, 52d, 53d, 105b, 115d, 129c, 135d, 140b, 149b–d, 152a–b, 153a–d, 158a, 165a, 168d, 175a, 179a–b, 180a, 180c–d, 184d, 186a, 189, 190, 191a–b, 192b, 194b–c, 197c, 198a–b, 199a–c, 205b–c, 210b, 213d, 215a, 215d, 221d, 222c, 223a–d, 224a–d, 225a–d, 226a–d, 231d, 233a, 233c, 246c, 248b, 248d, 278a–c, 288c, 294d, 305a–d, 306a, 307a–b.

P (script)—73c, 129b, 133c, 140a, 182b, 251a, 258a–c, 291d, 306b.

Palette—4a, 140a, 145b, 152a, 205a, 288d, 299b.

Panama—221d.

Parallelogram—9a.

Paris—182b.

Paris White (printed)—4b.

Peacock—123c–d, .

Pearl White (printed)—43a–b.

Pegasus—44b.

Pennant—15a–c, 104a.

Pgh. Pa.—291d.

Phoenix—8a–d, 10d.

Pike—209c, 210a.

Placard—85d, 131d, 133b, 136d, 165d, 167a–d, 169a, 171a, 206b, 207d.

Porcelain (printed)—10d, 16b, 29b–c, 31d, 33a–b, 38a–b, 44c, 53c, 107a–c, 164d, 180a, 188a–b, 194a, 211c–d, 213d, 215a–b, 245a, 277a.

Porcelaine Granite (printed)—110a.

Portland—192b.

Premium Granite (printed)—7b–c.

Premium Stone China (printed)—111a–c.

Princeton—105b, 175a.

Puerto Rico—241a, 242a–c, 243a, 243c–d, 244a.

Q (block print)—90, 129c.

Q (script)—77c.

Stone Ware (printed)—71b.

Stonewood, W. Va.—171a.

St. Paul—106c.

Stylized (shapes)—250a–c, 251b.

S-V (printed)—22a, 108b–c, 187c, 213c, 219a–b, 283c–d.

S-V China (printed)—25a, 108a.

S.V. China (printed)—28.

Swan—30c.

T (block print)—20c, 23b, 39b, 53d, 56d, 103a, 199c–d, 131c, 141a, 144d, 156a–c, 166d, 168a, 172a–c, 209b, 217b, 235b, 237a–b, 245a–c, 246a–c, 247a–d, 248a–d, 249a–d, 250a–b, 250d, 251a–c, 252a–c, 253a–d, 254a–d, 255a–d, 256a–d, 257a–d, 258a–d, 259a–c, 260a–c, 261b–d, 262a–d, 263a–d, 264a–d, 265a–c, 266a–c, 267d, 268a–d, 271a–d, 272a–c, 273a–d, 274a–d.

T (script)—26c, 134b–c, 159d, 255c.

Tableware (printed)—131c–d.

Tacoma—103a.

Texas—20c, 23b.

Trademark (printed)—7b–c, 8b–d, 35a–b, 60b, 65b–d, 100a, 101b, 130c, 168a–b, 284b–c, 297b–c.

Trade names (see listing under individual types).

Trent—271c.

Triangle—59a, 162a, 169a, 235c, 244b, 247b.

Turtle—131c.

U (block print)—45c, 54d, 106b, 175c, 213a, 217c, 243c–d, 275b, 276a.

Underglaze (printed)—26b–c, 46b–d, 85d, 87c, 91b–c, 121b, 135b, 157c, 158c, 200b, 203a–c, 204a, 206b–d, 207a–d, 208b–c, 216d, 253a, 273d.

Unicorn—11a, 13b–d, 30d, 31a–b, 97a, 163b–d, 178b, 179b, 181b, 186a–c, 191a–d, 211a, 227a, 269a, 270a–b, 275a, 284a, 297a.

U.S.A.—2a–b, 10d, 26b–c, 33a–b, 53a, 53d, 59d, 60d, 70b–c, 71b–c, 72a, 72c–d, 74a, 74c–d, 75c–d, 76a, 76d, 77a–d, 79a–b, 80b, 87a–c, 88d, 89c, 90a, 91a–c, 95, 107b, 117b–d, 118a–d, 119a–b, 120b–c, 121a–d, 122c–d, 126a–b, 127a–c, 129d, 130b, 130d, 132a, 132d, 133c–d, 134a, 135d, 137d, 139b, 139d, 140c, 141c, 142a–c, 143a–c, 144b, 145c, 146c, 151a–b, 152d, 159a, 167b, 168c, 171a, 190, 199b–c, 200a, 205a, 207a, 208d, 210a–b, 214c, 215b–d, 217c, 218a–d, 231c, 232a, 233b, 235c–d, 236b, 237a, 237c–d, 238b–c, 239a, 241a–c, 242a–c, 243a, 243c–d, 248c–d, 249a–c, 250a–b, 251c–d, 252a, 252c, 253a–b, 254a–c, 255c, 256a–c, 257a–b, 257d, 261d, 263a–c, 264a, 264d, 265a, 271a, 271c–d, 277a, 288a–b, 289b, 293a, 305c, 307c, (see also; made in U.S.A.).

Utah—106b.

V (block print)—15b, 29d, 36c, 46d, 96, 106a, 122a–b, 188a–b, 246a, 248c, 251b, 268b, 278d, 279d, 282a–c, 283a, 283c–d.

Victoria—36c.

Virginia—29d, 106a, 273b–c.

Vitreous (printed)—25b, 46b, 82a–d, 182a, 194a, 198a–b, 294c.

Vitrified (printed)—231a, 234c, 274a, 293a.

Vitrified China (printed)—166d, 168a–c, 229c, 231b–d, 232a.

ACKNOWLEDGEMENTS

This publication is the result of the cooperation and assistance of a great number of individuals, institutions, and organizations. Without the generous donation of photographic materials and technical guidance of Larry Walton, owner of the Camera Mart of East Liverpool, and his assistant, Mike Smith, the photographs of the pottery marks would not have been possible. If this manuscript could be dedicated it would be devoted to their efforts and support.

The physical preparation and mechanical compilation of a manuscript of this magnitude is never a singular effort. We consider ourselves fortunate to have numerous dedicated individuals assist us. The authors would particularly like to thank museum interpreter (East Liverpool Museum of Ceramics) Anne Vensel for her help in preparing the text and aiding in the compilation of the index of pottery marks. Special thanks are also extended to Gregory Shreve, Dean, Kent State University, Geauga Campus, and Michael A. Bertheaud, Educational Services Coordinator, Museum of Ceramics, for dealing with our inverted syntax, misplaced punctuation, and other grammatical oversights. Secretaries generally receive little credit for their efforts; we heartily thank Gladys Albaugh for her suggestions and for typing the manuscript. In addition, we thank Karen Russo for compiling the general index.

The process of locating and photographing examples of East Liverpool pottery and porcelain in museums, private collections, and at local potteries was a challenging task. We received a great deal of assistance in this area and are especially indebted to Bill Purton and Harriett Wilson and the Ohio Historical Society; Jack Lanam and the East Liverpool Historical Society; Woodrow Price, owner of the Quality Stamp Company; Susan Myers and Regina Lee Blaszcyk of the Smithsonian Institution; B. A. Wellman and Gus Gustafson of Buttzville Antique Center; George Miller of Parks Canada; Jo Cunningham of *The Glaze*; Michele Newton of the Degenhart Paperweight and Glass Museum; the Wellsville Historical Society; the Sebring Public Library; and Richard King, Dean, Kent State University, East Liverpool Campus. In addition to the above, we are grateful to the following individuals who made their collections available to us: Edna Miglore, Paul and Beth Dailey, Lois Kinsey, Joan Shreve, Grace Mahon, Margaret Rambo, R. Max Gard, Bob Barnhart, Betty Burch, Mrs. Dan McDonald, Ethel Preston, and Mrs. Kendall. All of the local potteries were most cooperative in locating and dating marks. For this help and information, we thank: Joseph Wells and Ed Carson of the Homer Laughlin China Company, Jack and Everson Hall of the Hall China Company, Terry and Tim O'Hara of the W. C. Bunting Company, John Gilkes of the Anchor Hocking Corporation (Taylor, Smith and Taylor), Harrison and Jay Keller of the Salem China Company, Bill Whiteman of the Sterling China Company, and John Briggs and Curt Fahnert of the Royal China Company.

We would also like to thank Don and Viktor Schreckengost, Harold (Skip) Dawson, Ronald L. Michael, and Roberta S. Greenwood for providing us with information, guidance, and encouragement. The authors are also grateful to Bob Duffy and Larry Hamilton of the Potter's Herald, Ray Schuck of the Allen County Historical Society, Christina Nelson of the Edison Institute, Lisa Taft of the American Ceramic Society, and Amos Loveday of the Ohio Historical Society. We would also like to recognize the contributions of the following individuals: Susan Weaver, Joseph Wagner Jr., Charles Lang, Jackman Vodrey, Bob Fryman, Linda DeLowry, W. T. Blake, H. A. Hoffman, Grace Burford, John Maltese and Ronald Fisher of Tri-state Publishing Company.

Index

www.ingramcontent.com/pod-product-compliance
Lightning Source LLC
Chambersburg PA
CBHW041109120626
46547CB00019B/2644